STORM
SIGNALS

Walter L. Gordon

STORM SIGNALS

New Economic Policies for Canada

McClelland and Stewart Limited

McClelland and Stewart Limited
The Canadian Publishers
25 Hollinger Road, Toronto.

0-7710-3436-9 paper bound
0-7710-3435-0 cloth bound

Printed and bound in Canada

Acknowledgements

I am extremely grateful to several of my friends who read all or parts of the text and gave me the benefit of their criticisms and suggestions. I shall not mention them by name in order to protect them from charges of "guilt by association." However, I am sure they know how much I appreciate their help.

Douglas Ross of the University of Toronto was of considerable assistance in the chapter on foreign policy, a subject in which he has exceptional knowledge and expertise. David Crane of *The Toronto Star* and several others were of great help to me in connection with the chapter on energy policy.

John L. Gordon made many valuable suggestions that I have incorporated in the text.

Tom McCormack, Susan Carter, and Edward Carrigan were helpful in research and checking references.

Diana Murray acted as general superintendent and coordinator of the project, as researcher, and in addition typed innumerable drafts. I am deeply grateful to her and to Dorothy Stuart who assisted with the typing.

Contents

STORM SIGNALS

Introduction

About twenty years ago, I prepared an article questioning the validity of some of Canada's accepted policies and recommending that a Royal Commission be established to consider them. At the time, the public mood and the economic outlook were euphoric. It was a period of apparently unlimited self-generating growth, of little or no thought about the future in specific terms, combined with a boundless optimism; a time of great confidence in the undeveloped but prospective riches from our natural resources and of extreme naiveté regarding foreign capital.

The Right Honourable C. D. Howe, Minister of Trade and Commerce, who had become the idol of most businessmen as a result of his great work in organizing production during World War II, saw no inherent danger in the continuing sales of Canada's resources and business enterprises to foreigners. He was inclined to encourage it. Mr. Howe was a very able man with a driving personality, but it was his nature to think of things in terms of their short term effects not of the implications for our longer term future.

Most businessmen felt Mr. Howe could do no wrong. Because of their ready access to him, they believed, and the general public believed, that the relationship of "business" with government was very close. This proximity had its advantages but, from a political point of view, may not have been entirely healthy. The voters may have sensed that this close association and the influence of big business with government was not necessarily in their best interest.

What troubled me especially, some twenty years ago, was the practice of selling Canada's resources and control of its industries to foreigners, usually American corporations. This practice was believed to be desirable because it brought with it access to U.S. management and technology, and often ensured access to markets. In my draft article (which was never published), I questioned this and many of the other policies and practices that had been developed and promoted by Mr. Howe, the most powerful of Prime Minister Louis St. Laurent's ministers.

During the early part of World War II, I had been a senior officer in the Department of Finance. Not wishing to embarrass my old associates there I sent a copy of the article to the Deputy Minister and asked whether its publication would upset things. Some weeks later, the Minister of Finance, the Honourable Walter Harris, telephoned. He had discussed my article with the Prime Minister, who liked the suggestion of a public review of existing economic and financial policies. Mr. Harris asked me whether, instead of publishing the article, he might use my ideas, including the proposal for a Royal Commission of Inquiry, in his forthcoming budget speech. Naturally, I agreed. Accordingly, in his budget speech a short time later, Mr. Harris announced that a Royal Commission was to be established. A few weeks after that, I was appointed Chairman of the Royal Commission on Canada's Economic Prospects. I should add that Mr. Howe was out of the country at the time and did not know about the Royal Commission. On his return, he made it clear that he was not at all pleased.

My first query to my fellow Commissioners – A.E. (Dal) Grauer, President of the B.C. Electric Company; Ray Gushue, President of Memorial University; Omer Lussier, a Quebec City forestry engineer; and Andrew Stewart, President of the University of Alberta – was a somewhat personal one: How long did they expect to live? None of them, in 1955, expected to live for more than another twenty years. To be on the safe side, we decided to give ourselves twenty-five years, and accordingly, all our forecasts were based on the year 1980. It would be up to others to explain any discrepancies between the forecasts and the actual results. However, only my friend Dal Grauer has died since the Commission was created. The other four of us are still here. Let me warn them we have only five years left.

The Commission's purpose was to forecast or to guess Canada's growth and development in the years ahead and, in that context, to suggest the kind of policies that might be required.

While the Commission's forecasts were based on 1980, they also indicated how things might look at five-year intervals. Comparisons between the forecasts to 1975 and the actual results to the end of 1974 are shown in Tables 1, 2 and 3.

Table 1
POPULATION – PERCENTAGE INCREASE

	Forecast	Actual
1955	100.0	100.0
1965	126.3	125.1
1970	140.5	135.7
1974		143.0
1975	156.2	

NOTE: The Commission's estimates were based on average immigration of 50,000, 75,000, and 100,000, respectively. Up to 1974, the actual average was 87,700. The latter figure has been used in the forecast above and in the forecast of the labour force in the table below:

Table 2
LABOUR FORCE – PERCENTAGE INCREASE

	Forecast	Actual
1955	100.0	100.0
1965	126.8	128.9
1970	144.2	153.1
1974		174.2
1975	162.7	

Table 3
GNP – PERCENTAGE INCREASE

	Forecast (low)	Forecast (high)	Actual
1955	100.0	100.0	100.0
1965	147.1	155.6	159.4
1970	183.5	199.9	201.4
1974			249.1
1975	222.8	251.4	

NOTE: The Commission's forecasts of GNP included two assumptions respecting "productivity." That is why there are two columns in the above table for the forecasts of GNP.

It would seem from these Tables that the Commission's highest forecast of GNP was very close to the actual results up to the end of 1974. Its forecast of population was a bit high, and of the labour force a bit low, but in neither case was it too far off the mark up to 1974.

So much for the forecasts, not by any means the most important part of their work in the view of the commissioners. The important part, in their opinion, was the more than fifty suggestions the Commission made about a variety of policies. One specific recommendation called for the creation of a national energy authority to advise the government on all matters relating to long-term energy requirements, export policy, and so on, and to approve all contracts or proposals respecting the export of energy sources. A new government was elected shortly after the Commission made this recommendation. The new Prime

Minister, the Right Honourable John G. Diefenbaker, was reluctant to accept the recommendation of a Royal Commission appointed by his predecessor. So he appointed a new Royal Commission under the chairmanship of Henry Borden to look into the energy question once again. The Borden Commission made essentially the same recommendation, and the National Energy Board was established. Most of the other policy proposals and suggestions made by the Royal Commission on Canada's Economic Prospects – with the notable exception of some very moderate suggestions relating to the foreign control of Canada's business enterprises and resources – have since been implemented in one way or another, many of them by the Liberal government under the Right Honourable Lester B. Pearson, which came to power in 1963.

As was to be expected, many changes have occurred in Canada and in the world since 1955 that could not have been foreseen at the time of the Commission. These included the world population explosion and an appreciation of its implications; the approaching end of a period of exponential rates of economic growth; the acute petroleum and other material shortages and the ability of the oil producing countries to get together in order to raise prices; the extent of the emergence of Japan and parts of Western Europe as rivals to U.S. industry; the rapid rise of the multinational corporations (largely American) and the implications of their growing power; the explorations in outer space and the new technology resulting from it; the widespread use of the birth control pill, its effect on population growth rates in the industrialized countries, and changes in sexual mores; the questioning of the work ethic and the rise of the hippy generation; and, finally, the demoralization of the United States due to all the foregoing, to the increasing affluence and power of the very rich, to the horrors of Vietnam, to the widespread corruption of the Nixon Administration, and its resulting loss of prestige and credibility in the world, if not in basic power. One can only add that politics and history are beset by the unexpected.

But despite the Commissioners' inability to foresee the various developments referred to – which would have required psychic qualities they did not possess – I believe the work of the Commission was very well worth while. For one thing, it encouraged Canadian businessmen to think and plan ahead, something few of them had done previously. Secondly, many policies have been changed or modified at least in part as a result of the suggestions made by the Commission. And thirdly, there was some tentative questioning, for the first time, of the presumed advantages of so much foreign control of the economy. The seeds sown by the Commission on this subject have taken many years to germinate and grow. But, at long last, they now show signs of developing into healthy plants. It seems fair to assert that a large majority of Canadians now realize that action must be taken if we are to regain our economic independence. It is only some of our politicians and perhaps some of the mandarins in Ottawa who have not yet caught up with the thinking of the general public on this vital issue.

Canada is faced with many problems at the present time among the most important being –

1. Unemployment at the highest level it has been in fourteen years.

2. Inflation which is eroding savings and creating a lack of confidence in the government's ability to manage the economy.

3. Current wage settlements that are aggravating inflation and also affecting our competitive position in export markets.

4. A huge deficit in our transactions with other countries on current account which is expected to amount to between $4 and $5 billion this year, an all-time record.

5. A steady increase in the control of Canadian resources and business enterprises by foreigners.

All these problems are interrelated and there is no simple panacea for resolving them. One thing is clear. The conventional economic antidotes that have been tried and tried again are out of date and ineffective. New policies and new approaches, geared more closely to the Canadian economy as it is today, are urgently required. I suggest the time has come, not for another Royal Commission or more inquiries into the foreign investment issue, but for some fundamental decisions about the kind of changes that are needed in Canada's economic policies. That is the purpose of this book. In it I shall try to paint with a broad brush leaving to experts on particular subjects the task of producing the refinements. The emphasis will be on the future, not the past.

Canadian economic policy must be considered in the light of present uncertain world conditions and, at least, the possibility that the whole international payments system could collapse. If that should happen, the Canadian Government would be forced to introduce controls it would much prefer to shy away from. Canadian policies must be considered also in the light of the relationship of the Canadian and U.S. economies. The first two chapters will deal with these matters – world conditions and the relationship of the Canadian and United States' economies. With this as background, I shall proceed to discuss some of the changes needed in Canadian economic policies.

"Seldom Seen,"   Walter L. Gordon
R.R. 3,   May, 1975
Schomberg, Ontario.

Chapter 1.

Canada's Position in a Troubled World

It is very easy these days to become pessimistic about the world outlook. One has only to read *The Limits to Growth*, published in October, 1972, as the first report to the Club of Rome, or Robert L. Heilbroner's *An Inquiry into the Human Prospect* (1974). These publications include some dire predictions about the rapid increase in world population, about the dismal prospects of feeding these increased multitudes, about the prices for oil and the limited quantities thereof, and about shortages of other industrial raw materials unless the industrialized nations can agree to reduce drastically their current exponential rates of economic growth.

Heilbroner warns us that if there is mass starvation and pestilence in the undeveloped countries, which may be inevitable if population in those areas continues to increase, this will lead to wars and revolutions, not to mention increased terrorist activities. When people have nothing to hope for and are starving, they may try to overthrow their leaders or to go to war with their neighbours no matter what the odds.

The first part of this chapter is based on a statement made by Walter L. Gordon at the 43rd Couchiching Conference August 10, 1974.

Moreover, some of the developing nations, including those in the Middle East, will soon have atomic weapons and may be prepared to use them if conflicts break out in their parts of the world. Heilbroner suggests that upheavals and wars in the developing and undeveloped nations, including the use of atomic weapons, will involve the industrialized nations, if only from a sense of self-preservation. He predicts that these circumstances, coupled with major shortages of industrial raw materials, will bring about authoritarian forms of government; democracy as we know it will not survive. He may be right.

Geoffrey Barraclough, writing in *The New York Review of Books* on January 23, 1975, puts forward a somewhat different thesis. He claims that most undeveloped countries could produce enough food for themselves and even for substantial increases in their populations if their arable land was used with this as the primary objective. This would mean converting their agriculture from the production of cash crops for export to food for home consumption, which is a much less profitable operation. Again, major changes in existing social structures, including land reform and the breaking up of present holdings, now in relatively few hands, would be inevitable. Whether this could be accomplished except under some form of authoritarian regime, as is the case in China, is extremely doubtful. And whether changes of this kind would be acceptable either to the countries concerned or to the Western nations is also questionable.

There can be no doubt that a tremendous increase will take place in world population by the end of the century. Even if enough food could be produced to feed these increased numbers, it is improbable that it could be delivered to all those who will need it. The difficulties are due to the weaknesses of organization and existing distribution facilities as well as corruption among those (including government officials) in charge of distribution. Corrupt and inefficient governments in the countries in question would have to be supplanted and new systems of land reform implemented and accepted. In addition, transportation and delivery systems would need to be increased and improved enormously. The costs would be tremendous. And if the populations of the undeveloped countries keep on growing after the turn of this century, the problem of feeding them could soon get out of hand. Containment of population growth by means of contraceptives is not likely to be more than marginally successful and there is little evidence to suggest that continence on a massive scale will be an acceptable alternative.

While it is horrible to say so, I am inclined to believe, as Heilbroner has suggested – and contrary to Barraclough's more optimistic view of the possible – that the undeveloped countries have before them the spectre of starvation on a massive scale, of plagues, and of war. While both the developed and the developing countries should do whatever may be practicable to alleviate the situation, the magnitude of the problem should be acknowledged. It is a frightening prospect.

For their part, the industrialized nations are unlikely to agree to a *voluntary* slowing down of their own rates of economic growth to any meaningful degree. There will be disruptions in their economies, that much seems certain. The oil crisis, for example, may force involuntary slowdowns in the rates of economic growth of some countries. As other materials become in short supply, other disruptions may follow. But for some time, industry in many industrialized nations can be counted on to find substitutes or partial substitutes, or to develop alternative approaches.

This is what modern technology and modern industry are all about. The compelling urge of industrialists and businessmen to expand, to grow, to make more money, should not be underestimated. That is the essence of the capitalist system. And while enlightened citizens in the developed nations – especially the younger members of society – are questioning the current worship of an ever-rising GNP (the measurement of a nation's total output of goods and services) as the end we should all strive for, it will take many years before we are likely to settle for new objectives.

In the meantime, however, it is possible that the whole house of cards could fall to the ground as the result of a breakdown of the vitally important international payments system that many people have tended to take for granted, except perhaps in wartime. The leading article in the January 1975 issue of *Foreign Affairs* deals with this question in some detail. The article was written by a group of five well qualified individuals—Khodadad Farmanfarmaian, formerly Governor of the Central Bank of Iran, Armin Gutowski, Member of the Council of Economic Experts on Economic Development in West Germany, Saburo Okita, Chairman of the Japan Economic Research Centre, Robert V. Roosa, former Under Secretary of the U.S. Treasury for Monetary Affairs, and Carroll L. Wilson of the Massachusetts Institute of Technology.

The article discusses the sharp price increases imposed by the Organization of Oil Producing Countries (OPEC) a year earlier – increases that stabilized by late in 1974 at approximately ten dollars a barrel, or about four times the mid-1973 price. Subject to certain conditions, the authors estimate that over the five years 1975 to 1979 inclusive, the oil importing countries of the world will pay these OPEC countries a total of at least $600 billion (in 1974 dollars). This would present a huge transfer problem. They believe that while conservation of energy or conversion to alternative fuels can be useful, this will not help very much in the next five years. Lead times for new developments are just too long. Nor do they believe that increased trade with the OPEC countries can solve the problem. They claim there are limits to the amount of imports of goods and services the OPEC countries can absorb. And they question whether the banking systems in some of the importing countries can handle the huge balances that will need to be invested in such countries.

So far, the problem of the recycling of "petro dollars" has been less traumatic than the authors of the article predicted. This is due to the continuance of lower imports by the oil importing countries as a result of the world-wide re-concession, of conservation measures and of climatic conditions. It is due also to the fact that the OPEC countries have been able to absorb huge imports, including weapons and war materials, and to make very considerable loans and investments abroad. This has led some analysts to believe the problem of the oil producers' surplus earnings will not be as serious as the *Foreign Affairs* article suggested. But most of the factors cited above are temporary or limited in their application. A solution to the world's international payments difficulties has not yet been found. It follows, therefore, that the problem represented by these huge recycling processes may hang over our heads for several years at least.

Apart altogether from the possibility of a breakdown of the international payments system, there is the continuing danger of war in the Middle East between Israel and the Arab States. Iran and the Arab States are in the process of acquiring modern arms. They will soon be very powerful as well as very rich. If the United States and the Soviet Union could get together and guarantee Israel's boundaries, peace might be ensured. But if the two super-powers are on opposite sides of a conflict between the Arabs and the Jews, then anything could happen.

Having painted this drear and gloomy picture, let me add my hope, I hesitate to say belief, that the dire events discussed in this chapter may not occur, at least insofar as the Western World is concerned – or at any rate not quite as soon as some forecasters predict. We can hope that a major war in the Middle East, or anywhere else, will be avoided. I have referred to the ability of modern industry to find substitutes for materials in short supply and different ways of doing things. While it is probably too late to stop the world population from doubling by the year 2000, the two super-powers and the other industrialized nations (or some of them) may manage to remain reasonably prosperous for another several decades after that, perhaps even for another century. But only if – and it is a big if – they can get along among themselves and if they can resolve their energy and international payments difficulties.

In considering the problems of this troubled world, there is another factor to be considered: the widening gap between the rich and poor. There is the gulf between the rich and the poor nations, the latter with their millions of people trying to subsist on annual incomes of $100 or $200 or less. The implications of a continuance of this disparity have been touched on very briefly in the preceding pages.

But even in the wealthiest nation of all, the United States, there are wide differences between the rich and powerful and those at the lower levels of the economic scale. The rapid rise of the multinational corporations since World War II, a large majority of which have their headquarters in the United States, has placed immense power in the hands of a relatively few senior financiers and businessmen. If continued, this development could become very disturbing to the general public.

Canadians are more aware than they used to be of the power and influence wielded by these multinational corporations and the men who direct them and their subsidiaries in this country. More Americans, for their part, are beginning to realize the extent to which the senior executives of multinational corporations based in the United States can influence the economy of their own country and the lives of the workers they employ. For example, the multinationals tend to shift production to countries with much lower wage rates than those prevailing in the United States.* This means loss of jobs at home.

The motives of the top executives who make such decisions are based primarily, if not entirely, on maximizing the profits of their world-wide corporations. They are responsible to no one except, perhaps theoretically, to their shareholders, and governments seem powerless or at least unwilling to interfere. As the multinationals become ever larger, the influence of their top executives will increase proportionately. It could mean quite literally that a few hundred individuals will soon become more powerful than are many governments. Furthermore, there can be no certainty that such power will be used to the best advantage of all the people concerned. The alleged activities of I.T. & T.'s subsidiaries in Chile aimed at the overthrow of the late President Allende are a case in point. Was it in the best interests of the Chilean people as a whole to bring about the overthrow of their duly elected president even if he was a Marxist? Is the present military dictatorship in that country an improvement? Canadians would be naive to believe that the top executives of multinational corporations with subsidiaries in Canada would refrain, or in the past have refrained, from exerting influence on the policies of this country.

Compared with that of many other countries, Canada's position in the years ahead should be relatively favourable.

---

* See a two-part article by Richard Bonet and Ronald Muller in the December 2 and December 9, 1974, issues of *The New Yorker*.

We should not have a population problem or a food shortage. We are blessed with at least some, if not all, the energy sources and industrial raw materials we need. While, according to most recent estimates, we have only limited reserves of oil and natural gas, at least until we can develop the tar sands and discover more oil in the Far North, we do have some alternatives such as coal and uranium (provided of course that we decide to safeguard our reserves of uranium before it is too late). It follows that for some years into the future, the Canadian economy should continue to grow. But quite probably this will be at a more modest rate than in the past; and it will have its downs as well as ups.

Canadians are not quite so wedded to a system of uncontrolled "free enterprise" as our friends to the south of us, which may be to our advantage. Canada has a mixed enterprise economy now and if it becomes necessary from time to time for our governments to intervene still further in its workings, most Canadians will probably accept this. It will not be easy for us, however, to retain our independence as a separate sovereign state in a dangerous and uncertain world. It never has been. We shall have to reconcile regional differences and objectives within our own country. It is axiomatic that we must remain united. If some provinces were to separate that would mean the end of Canada. One of our major problems will be our relations with the United States as that country runs short of raw materials and is tempted to rely more and more on Canada to help meet its needs. This will call for determination and skilful diplomacy on our part.

There is no doubt we shall have our problems, very serious ones. But Canada has a majority government at present which is something in our favour. (It remains to be seen whether we have a government that is wise and strong enough to do the things that will be necessary, some of which will be unpopular.) While, therefore, no one can fail to be pessimistic about the future of the world society,

Canadians can take some comfort from the fact that, assuming our national affairs are well handled, we may be in a more favourable position than most other countries.

Chapter 2

Canada's Position vis-à-vis the United States

Canada is a great trading nation with a very open economy. One of our country's strengths and at the same time one of its weaknesses is its proximity to the United States and thus its access (albeit limited and restricted) to the greatest market in the world. But before discussing the amount and the nature of Canada's trade with the United States, it may be helpful to indicate the size of our trade with the world as a whole and then go on to show how much of this total is with the United States.

Our trade balances and deficits or surpluses on Current Account with all countries over the past few years are set forth in Table 4.

We had an over-all surplus in merchandise trade with the rest of the world in every one of the past five years, but a deficit on Current Account in the last three of these years. In 1974 the deficit came close to $2 billion, and in 1975 it may amount to between $4 and $5 billion.

This record deficit in our balances with other countries poses a very serious problem for Canada. It will mean high levels of unemployment. It will bring about a reduction in the exchange rate for the Canadian dollar. The fall in the exchange rate which began in May, 1975, while this book was being written, will probably continue in the months

Table 4
CANADA'S BALANCE OF PAYMENTS ON CURRENT
ACCOUNT
1965-1974

(millions of dollars)

Year	Merchandise			Service and Transfer Items (Net)	Balance on Current Account	Percentage of Mdse. Exports to GNP
	Exports	Imports	Balance			
1965	$ 8,745	$ 8,627	$ 118	$-1,248	$-1,130	15.8%
1970	16,921	13,869	3,052	-1,946	1,106	19.7
1971	17,961	15,534	2,427	-2,121	306	19.2
1972	20,222	18,577	1,645	-2,300	- 655	19.5
1973	25,500	23,269	2,231	-2,656	- 425	21.4
1974	32,493	31,473	1,020	-2,897	-1,877	23.3

ahead. Devaluation should be welcomed, because eventually a lower value for the Canadian dollar will tend to stimulate the economy and provide more job opportunities. But in the meantime, it will have an adverse effect on the cost of living.

About two-thirds of our exports over the years, as shown in Table 5, have gone to the United States and about the same high proportion of our imports have come from there.

Usually, our Current Account deficits with the United States were financed in part by our Current Account surpluses with *other* countries and by capital inflows and changes in our exchange reserves. But in 1974, Canada had a small deficit in her transactions with other countries as well as a huge deficit with the United States ($1,812 million).

Canada's major exports are farm products (including wheat), base metals, forest products (including newsprint), and crude oil and natural gas offset partially by imports of petroleum products. Our imports consist of motor vehicles and parts, which recently have been offset to a considerable extent by exports of similar goods. Although, as shown in Table 5, we have had a favourable balance in our merchandise trade in recent years, a large part of our exports have been in the form of industrial raw materials with a relatively low labour content, while our imports for the most part are manufactured goods having a high labour content. This makes it more difficult to maintain high levels of employment in Canada.

A more detailed analysis of Canadian-United States trade in finished goods shows that by far the largest single item is automobiles and parts. To increase the production of North American-style cars in Canada and thus reduce the trade imbalance with the United States, the Canadian Government negotiated the auto pact with that country in 1964-65. The result was a considerable expansion of the au-

Table 5
CANADA'S BALANCE OF PAYMENTS ON CURRENT
ACCOUNT WITH THE UNITED STATES
1965-1974

(millions of dollars)

Year	Merchandise			Service and Transfer Items (Net)	Deficit on Current Account	Percentage of Total	
	Exports	Imports	Balance			Mdse. Exports	Mdse. Imports
1965	$ 4,993	$ 6,034	$-1,041	$- 896	$-1,937	57%	70%
1970	10,959	9,838	1,121	-1,286	- 165	65	71
1971	12,082	10,873	1,209	-1,491	- 282	67	70
1972	14,025	12,792	1,233	-1,687	- 454	69	69
1973	17,253	16,439	814	-2,071	-1,257	68	71
1974	21,590	21,065	525	-2,337	-1,812	66	67

tomotive industry in this country; hence a considerable increase in employment opportunities. In ten years, the value of total production in Canada increased enormously; our trade position in automotive products with the United States improved spectacularly, from a deficit of $711 million in 1965 to a surplus of $230 million in 1971. The latter figure was achieved, in part, however, by a cyclical and temporary factor.

In 1970, the recession hit Canada and the United States at about the same time, but it affected sales here more than in the U.S. Partly because of this, in 1970, our imports of automotive products declined by $213 million (as compared with 1969), while our exports of parts increased by $100 million. Our total surplus for 1970, including vehicles and parts was $204 million. As already noted, it reached $230 million in 1971; then dropped to $67 million the following year.

Since 1972, our position has worsened; the deficit with the United States in automobiles and parts in 1973 was $440 million. This increased to $1.3 billion in 1974. Here again, a cyclical factor was present. This time the recession started earlier in the United States and hit much harder than in Canada. Partly as a consequence, our total exports increased by only $125 million in 1974 and our imports rose by $1 billion.

These recent developments cannot be explained by cyclical factors only. An American group of auto-industry analysts, including John Kolozsi of the Bank of America, forecasts a long-term slowdown in the rate of growth of car sales in the United States caused by the declining birth rate and a greater emphasis on mass transportation. The group also predicts that foreign cars will get a greater share of the American market until the U.S. industry has adjusted to the new consumers' psychology. According to this forecast, American production will not return to the level attained in 1973 until 1983, and it will put more emphasis on small cars.

The same basic trends affecting demand are developing in Canada and for the same reasons. As a result, our trade position with countries other than the United States in automotive products has steadily worsened since the end of 1968. Our deficit with these countries, only $16 million in 1965, reached $484 million in 1974. Japan has become our second largest automobile supplier after the United States.

These developments do not augur well for Canada. If American production puts more emphasis on small cars to meet the requirements of this growing market in both the United States and Canada, and if Canadian subsidiaries are not allowed to make similar adjustments, Canadian production will be restricted to big cars, representing the shrinking portion of the North American market. In such circumstances our trade position in automotive products would continue to worsen, not only with the United States, but also with the rest of the world.

If it is determined that long-term factors are changing the trade patterns between the two countries and are contributing significantly to a chronic and growing deficit for Canadian trade in automotive products, the government should review the situation very carefully and initiate negotiations without delay to modify the auto pact. In the meantime, the Canadian automobile manufacturers should be urged to develop more sources for parts and components in Canada and to import less from other countries, the United States in particular.

Partly because of what happened in the automotive industry in the last two years, and partly because of increased service charge payments by Canadian subsidiaries to their foreign parents, our deficit on current account with the United States increased considerably in 1974 and will increase again in

1975. It is most unwise for Canada to continue to incur deficits on Current Account with other nations, primarily with the United States, year after year. The fact that we have been doing so for decades does not mean this has been in our best interests. It has not.

As reported by the United States Department of Commerce, Canadian subsidiaries of United States parent corporations buy considerably more parts and components from their parent corporations than do similar subsidiaries in other countries. The presumption is that foreign-controlled Canadian subsidiary companies are importing parts and components that could be produced in Canada. If this were done, employment in Canada would be increased. Government authorities should discuss this matter, not only with the automobile manufacturers, but with all the larger foreign-controlled manufacturing companies in Canada, and urge them to develop alternative sources of supply in Canada for the parts and components they are presently importing. If the companies in question will do this voluntarily, so much the better. If not, the government should seek legislation that would permit its officials to monitor the operations of foreign-controlled Canadian manufacturing concerns and, where it seemed desirable, to instruct them to do so. All arrangements whether voluntary or formal, should include requests to such companies as Ford of Canada to re-establish complete purchasing departments in this country.

The amount of service charges of all kinds paid by Canadian subsidiaries to their foreign parent corporations is reported to have increased considerably in recent years. If this is so, the Department of National Revenue should be instructed to examine these various charges carefully and to place strict limits on the amounts thereof that may be deducted for Canadian tax purposes in the future.

Another and most effective way of bringing our Current Account transactions with the United States into better balance would be to encourage a reduction in the value of the Canadian dollar compared with the u.s. dollar. In view of our increasing deficit on Current Account with other countries, especially the United States, this will probably happen in any event. Reducing interest rates in Canada closer to those prevailing in the United States would be one way to encourage this objective. Presumably, this would bring about a withdrawal of funds from Canada and thus a downward pressure on the exchange rate. In addition, it may be necessary for the Bank of Canada to monitor and control the timing of the large-scale inflows of capital required for such projects as the James Bay development and the various projected pipe lines.

In considering the implications of a reduced exchange rate for the Canadian dollar, one should recall that our dollar was pegged at 90.9 u.s. cents from 1939 to 1946 and at 92.5 u.s. cents from 1962 to 1970. This worked to our advantage.

Before leaving the problem of our over-all balance of payments, I should like to mention another matter that has an indirect bearing on the subject of this chapter. It is in Canada's interests to expand its foreign trade, and diversify it to the fullest extent possible. But if we wish to develop trade with the Arab countries and with some of those in Eastern Europe and elsewhere, we should pay more attention to the way in which they are accustomed to conduct their own affairs. For example, it would be easier for some of them, and better understood by them, if the Canadian Government were to establish a national trading corporation. The trade officials of the countries mentioned could deal directly with this one body, rather than with perhaps several hundred separate Canadian corporations. The proposed national trading corporation would act on behalf of Canadian manufacturers and producers if they so wished. In trade, it is a good maxim that proclaims the customer is always right, not only as to the kind and style of goods he wants to buy but also as to the channels through which they are presented to him.

Given the size of our trade with the U.S., a high degree of integration of our economies is inevitable, but this integration is reinforced and tightened by U.S. control of a great many Canadian business enterprises and resources. Some seven or eight thousand Canadian corporations are controlled by foreigners, mostly enterprising Americans or their corporations. The number of the largest Canadian companies in some of the more dynamic industries that are controlled abroad is of even more significance. In August 1974, *The Financial Post* published a list of the one hundred largest manufacturing, resource, and utility companies in Canada according to volume of sales. The list did not include Canadian International Paper, which is provincially incorporated and whose figures are not available, nor the various Canadian interests of I.T. & T., which are not consolidated. If these two companies are added to the list, we find 61 foreign-controlled companies among Canada's largest corporations.

As shown in Table 6, 61 of the 102 largest Canadian corporations in the manufacturing, resource and utility fields are controlled directly or indirectly from abroad. As has been said so often, no other country in the industrialized world has allowed so much of its industry, and so much of its natural resources, to be controlled by foreigners.

Canada's expenditures on defence ($2,350 million in 1974-75) are relatively small by international standards; nevertheless our defence forces work closely with the United States, especially in NORAD – yet another factor that ties our two countries together. There is also the Defence Production Sharing Agreement with the United States which was originally conceived to encourage exports from Canada to about balance our imports of defence materials. While the amounts involved are not large in the context of our total trade, this agreement was an embarrassment during the Vietnam war. It was said that while Canada claimed to be neutral in that conflict, nevertheless Canadians were profiting from it. This was true. I would like to see the Defence Production Sharing Agreement abrogated in order to avoid the possibility of finding ourselves in a similar embarrassing position at some time in the future.

Taken altogether, the Canadian and United States economies are linked to a much greater extent than many Canadians fully realize. Canada is the biggest customer of the United States and u.s. investments in Canada are greater than they are in any other country. The total book value of all u.s. direct investments abroad in August 1974 was $107,268 million. Of this, $28,055 million, or more than twenty-five per cent, was invested in Canada. (The next highest was $11,115 million invested in the United Kingdom.) The present day value of these investments may be appreciably greater.

In view of these huge investments in Canada – and quite apart from our mutual interest in defence – it is understandable that the u.s. Government should take more than a passing interest in Canadian economic policies and exercise considerable influence thereon.

Many, if not most, Canadians have friends and relatives or business associates in the United States, and these relationships are usually warm and intimate. At government levels, u.s. and Canadian officials usually get on well together. After all, we speak the same language and our points of view are usually much the same; we are allies in a troubled world; and our two countries are both relatively prosperous.

But it would be unwise for Canadians to take too much

THE SIXTY-ONE LARGEST MANUFACTURING, RESOURCE, AND UTILITY COMPANIES IN CANADA THAT WERE CONTROLLED ABROAD IN 1974

SALES 000's	COMPANY	ASSETS 000's	CONTROLLED BY
	Oil and Gas		
$2,580,000	Imperial Oil	$2,132,000	69.4% Exxon Corp., U.S.A.
1,077,890	Shell Canada	1,195,851	71% Royal Dutch/Shell Group
1,032,410	Gulf Oil Canada	1,367,287	68.3% Gulf Oil Corp., U.S.A.
558,183	Texaco Canada	500,290	68.2% Texaco Inc., U.S.A.
335,692	Petrofina Canada	405,557	71.8% Petrofina S.A., Belgium
311,044	BP Canada	443,288	65.6% British Petroleum Co., England
252,598	Husky Oil Co.	320,174	20.7% G.E. Nielson & Associates, U.S.A.
192,604	Amoco Canada	511,391	100% Standard Oil of Indiana, U.S.A.
164,507	Texaco Explorations Canada	447,765	100% Texaco Inc., U.S.A.
164,222	Pacific Petroleums	528,371	48.4% Phillips Petroleum, U.S.A.
141,893	Sun Oil Co.	239,270	100% Sun Oil Co., U.S.A.
136,417	Hudson's Bay Oil & Gas	401,394	53.1% Continental Oil, U.S.A.
133,916	Canadian Hydrocarbons Ltd.	177,623	51.9% – U.S.A. 17.7% Europe 34.2%
	Pipe Lines		
202,831	Interprovincial Pipe Line	620,260	32.9% Imperial Oil which in turn is controlled by Exxon Corp., U.S.A.
168,814	Westcoast Transmission	614,217	14.8% Phillips Petroleum Co., U.S.A. 31% Pacific Petroleum which in turn is 48.4% owned by Phillips Petroleum, U.S.A., 15%

Mining

Company			Ownership
Falconbridge Nickel	438,163	742,337	19.7% Superior Oil, U.S.A. McIntyre Mines owns 36.9%; 53.3% of McIntyre is owned by Superior Oil, U.S.A.
Rio Algom	314,920	416,620	51.3% Rio-Tinto-Zinc Corp., England
Hudson Bay Mining & Smelting	182,385	278,852	34.7% Anglo American Group, S. Africa
Canadian Johns-Manville	140,406	206,847	100% Johns-Manville Corp., U.S.A.

Forest Products

Company			Ownership
Canadian International Paper	n.a.	n.a.	100% International Paper Corp., U.S.A.
Crown Zellerbach Canada	297,246	263,754	89.8% Crown Zellerbach, U.S.A.
Weldwood of Canada	265,374	179,878	73.6% Champion International Corp., U.S.A.
B.C. Forest Products	253,603	316,761	41.8% Mead Corp., Scott Paper, U.S.A.
Reed Paper Ltd.	217,568	214,620	100% Reed Paper Group, England

Automotive, etc.

Company			Ownership
Ford Motor Company of Canada	$3,594,300	$1,284,800	88% Ford Motor Co., U.S.A.
General Motors of Canada	3,116,092	916,554	100% General Motors Corp., U.S.A.
Chrysler Canada	1,695,140	454,526	100% Chrysler Corp., U.S.A.
International Harvester of Canada	466,877	170,639	100% International Harvester, U.S.A.
Ensite Ltd	370,506	154,444	100% Ford Motor Co., U.S.A.
Goodyear Tire Canada	239,988	161,108	87.4% Goodyear Tire & Rubber, U.S.A.
American Motors (Canada)	223,690	34,157	100% American Motors, U.S.A.
Uniroyal Ltd.	189,494	114,162	100% Uniroyal Inc., U.S.A.
Firestone of Canada	171,781	154,357	100% Firestone Tire & Rubber, U.S.A.
White Motor of Canada	168,095	70,803	100% White Motor Corp., U.S.A.
Budd Automotive of Canada	134,662	87,813	81.5% The Budd Co., U.S.A.

SALES 000's	COMPANY	ASSETS 000's	CONTROLLED BY
	Computers		
517,855	IBM Canada	362,480	100% IBM, U.S.A.
	Chemicals		
383,289	Canadian Industries Ltd.	301,467	73.3% Imperial Chemical Industries, England
306,361	Dupont of Canada	252,785	74.9% Dupont, U.S.A.
245,688	Union Carbide, Canada	229,665	75.0% Union Carbide Corp., U.S.A.
195,000	Dow Chemical of Canada	217,000	100% Dow Chemical, U.S.A.
	Tobacco		
466,563	Imasco Ltd.	293,880	53.0% England
372,706	Rothmans of Pall Mall Canada	452,123	59.2% Rembrandt Controlling Investments Ltd., S. Africa
	Foods, etc.		
403,876	Swift Canadian Co.	99,152	100% Swift & Co., U.S.A.
266,127	Maple Leaf Mills	139,213	73.7% Norris Grain Co., U.S.A.
212,947	Kraft Foods Ltd.	89,972	100% Kraftco Corp., U.S.A.
212,758	General Foods Ltd.	116,248	100% General Foods Corp., U.S.A.
207,034	Continental Can of Canada	136,257	100% Continental Can, U.S.A.
186,918	Lever Brothers Ltd.	87,429	100% Unilever Ltd., England
184,698	Standard Brands Ltd.	143,989	100% Standard Brands Inc., U.S.A.
161,673	Robin Hood Multifoods Ltd.	73,593	100% International Multifoods, U.S.A.

Miscellaneous

$583,414	Canadian General Electric	$ 429,720	91.8% General Electric, U.S.A.
509,589	Genstar Ltd.	501,302	33.4% – Belgium 22.4%; Britain 11%
336,276	Westinghouse Canada	181,435	75.4% Westinghouse Electric, U.S.A.
326,637	Anglo-Canadian Telephone	1,145,884	84.0% General Telephone & Electric, U.S.A.
276,327	Canada Cement Lafarge	403,834	54.5% Ciments Lafarge, France
253,628	Hawker Siddeley Canada Ltd.	225,874	59.2% Hawker Siddeley Group, England
220,741	Celanese Canada	214,823	56.7% Celanese Corp., U.S.A.
169,915	R.C.A. Ltd.	109,275	100% R.C.A. Corp., U.S.A.
154,549	Rockwell International of Canada	72,532	100% Rockwell International Corp., U.S.A.
138,350	Kodak Canada Ltd.	107,843	100% Eastman Kodak Co., U.S.A.
n.a.	I.T. & T. Canadian interests	n.a.	100% I.T. & T., U.S.A.

for granted. Some U.S. officials or ex-officials look forward to the day when Canada will become part of the U.S. This is what George Ball, Under Secretary of State under Presidents Kennedy and Johnson, had to say in his book, *The Discipline of Power*, published in 1968:

> Canada, I have long believed, is fighting a rearguard action against the inevitable. Living next to our nation, with a population ten times as large as theirs and a gross national product fourteen times as great, the Canadians recognize their need for United States capital; but at the same time they are determined to maintain their economic and political independence. Their position is understandable, and the desire to maintain their national integrity is a worthy objective. But the Canadians pay heavily for it and, over the years, I do not believe they will succeed in reconciling the intrinsic contradiction of their position. I wonder, for example, if the Canadian people will be prepared indefinitely to accept, for the psychic satisfaction of maintaining a separate national and political identity, a per capita income less than three-fourths of ours. The struggle is bound to be a difficult one – and I suspect, over the years, a losing one. Meanwhile there is danger that the efforts of successive Canadian governments to prevent United States economic domination will drive them toward increasingly restrictive nationalistic measures that are good neither for Canada nor for the health of the whole trading world.
>
> Thus, while I can understand the motivating assumptions of the Canadian position, I cannot predict a long life-expectancy for her present policies. The great land mass to the south exerts an enormous gravitational attraction while at the same time tending to repel, and even without the divisive element of a second culture in Quebec, the resultant strains and pres-

sures are hard to endure. Sooner or later, commercial imperatives will bring about free movement of all goods back and forth across our long border; and when that occurs, or even before it does, it will become unmistakably clear that countries with economies so inextricably intertwined must also have free movement of the other vital factors of production – capital, services and labour. The result will inevitably be substantial economic integration, which will require for its full realization a progressively expanding area of common political decision.

Since George Ball expressed these views, the GNP per capita in Canada has been growing more rapidly than that of the United States. In 1974 the Canadian figure had risen to 94.3 per cent of that in the United States, so his argument has even less validity in strictly economic terms than when he wrote his book. Despite this, I believe Canadians should take the views of people like George Ball very seriously. Here is a man who was a senior and influential member of two U.S. Administrations. It was strongly rumoured that he would become Secretary of State if Hubert Humphrey won the 1968 presidential election. He leaves no doubt about his view as to Canada's place in the world of the future.

Other U.S. officials regard Canada as a kind of colony available to be exploited, no doubt in a kindly way, when and if occasion arises. When the U.S. finds itself in difficulties and decides to take action, we should not expect its officials to worry too much about the side effects of such actions on other countries – including Canada. They are not likely to do so. Let me cite three examples that have happened in the past. In July 1963, President Kennedy announced his intention to ask Congress to approve the Interest Equalization Tax. Its effect would have been to make it much more costly for Canadians (including Canadian provincial governments) to borrow in the New York Market. The result would have been chaos in Canadian capital markets and a forced devaluation of the currency, the second devaluation in a little over a year. The implications were pointed out at once to U.S. Secretary of the Treasury, Douglas Dillon. He was impressed and persuaded President Kennedy to exempt Canada from the legislation. This was announced immediately and panic was avoided. On that occasion, we were lucky.

Late in 1965, again because of balance of payments problems, the U.S. government issued guidelines to corporations with subsidiaries in other countries. Exports to such subsidiaries were to be stepped up; dividends to U.S. corporations by their foreign subsidiaries were to be increased and idle cash balances repatriated. In speaking about these guidelines, Henry Fowler, who by that time had succeeded Douglas Dillon as Secretary of the Treasury, referred to the role of multinational companies (that is, American corporations with subsidiaries in other countries): these companies "have not only a commercial importance – but a highly significant role in a United States foreign policy that has met with general approval by the Atlantic countries." I do not know about the approval of the Atlantic countries other than Canada, but there is no doubt these guidelines created serious balance of payments difficulties for our country.

The third example is the various measures introduced by President Nixon in August 1971. These included a surcharge on imports into the United States (not including imports under the auto pact) and incentives for increased exports from the United States. Canada asked to be exempted but was refused.

The fact is that because of the close integration of our economies, Canada is very vulnerable to changes in U.S. policies. There was a time some years ago when we hoped for, and often received, special treatment if we expected to be hurt by U.S. policies. But those days are over. It follows, therefore, that we should do whatever we can to protect ourselves against sudden shifts in U.S. policies. It should be Canada's firm objective, gradually but persistently, to free ourselves, at least to an extent, from the sometimes overpowering embraces of our southern friend.

Chapter 3.

The Structure
of Canadian Industry

John Kenneth Galbraith, the ex-Canadian Harvard economist, writer, lecturer, debater, one-time U.S. Ambassador to India, and top-level adviser to Democratic presidential candidates, has done more than anyone else to describe the present structure of U.S. industry with its increasing concentration in monopolies and oligopolies*. Anyone who has read Galbraith knows the "unseen hand" in "the market place" that was supposed to control the supply and the prices of the things we buy no longer applies to most consumer goods.

To put this another way, Adam Smith's precepts about prices being set through free competition in the market place are out of date when it comes to many of the things on which we spend a large part of our incomes – automobiles, electrical appliances, household furnishings, gasoline, fuel oil, liquor, clothing, much of the food we buy from the supermarkets, pharmaceuticals, and a host of other items. In these cases, it is the manufacturers who, through advertising, create the demand for their products and who establish the prices.

Suppose, for example, some large pharmaceutical com-

*See in particular Galbraith's *The New Industrial State*, (1967), and his *Economics and the Public Purpose*, (1974).

pany decides to promote a new brand of hair spray. The company may launch a massive advertising campaign designed to create a demand for this particular product. Or consider General Motors faced with the public interest in small foreign cars. No doubt, the company wished to create a demand for American-made models of a similar type. Accordingly, it produced the Vega. After seeing this automobile in endless commercials, usually accompanied by an attractive and expensive-looking female, many men are enticed into buying one even though they know full well that the girl in the advertisements will not be included in the package. In such cases, the classical economic theory of the market place no longer has much validity. It is the powerful corporation that decides what it wants to produce and then proceeds to create the demand for it. Moreover, the more important industries are often dominated by one or two or three companies. These companies exert a major influence in establishing the selling prices for their products.

The market place theory of competition still applies, of course, to many items – to those sold by the corner groceries (that still struggle against the competition of the chain stores), to some such individual service people as gardeners, undertakers, tailors, repairmen, hairdressers, and, as Galbraith sometimes points out, practitioners of the oldest of the professions. But these things are of less importance in terms of total consumer expenditures than the others I have mentioned.

The same situation exists in Canada. A great many of our important industries are now dominated by monopolies or oligopolies that not only decide what to produce, but also proceed to create a demand for their products. At the same time, while it is against the law for the principal companies to get together and set prices, it is pretty well acknowledged, at least in business circles, that the dominant company in any particular industry can exert great influence by what is euphemistically called "price leadership."

Some of the important industries in Canada that over the years have developed along monopolistic or oligopolistic lines (many of whose principal companies are controlled abroad) are set out in Table 7.

Table 7
SOME CANADIAN MONOPOLIES AND OLIGOPOLIES

Petroleum	* Imperial Oil
	* Gulf Canada
	* Shell Canada
	* Texaco Canada
	* BP Canada
Mining	International Nickel
	* Falconbridge Nickel
	Noranda Mines
	* Hudson Bay Mining & Smelting
	* Rio Algom
Forest Products	* Canadian International Paper
	Abitibi and its subsidiary
	Price Co.
	MacMillan Bloedel
	* Crown Zellerbach, Canada
Automobiles	* General Motors of Canada
	* Ford of Canada
	* Chrysler of Canada
Computers	* IBM Canada
Steel	Steel Co. of Canada
	Dofasco
	Algoma Steel
Aluminum	Alcan Aluminum
Liquor	Seagrams
	Hiram Walker-Gooderham & Worts
Beer	Labatt's
	Molson's
	* Carling O'Keefe
Tobacco	* IMASCO
	* MacDonald's Tobacco
	* Rothman's

Banking	Royal
	Commerce
	Montreal
	Nova Scotia
	Toronto Dominion
**Telephones	Bell Canada
**Railways	Canadian National
	Canadian Pacific
**Airlines	Air Canada
	CP Air

*Controlled abroad.

**Rates approved by Canadian Transport Commission.

Long ago, it was decided that the rates charged by public utilities – the railroads and other forms of public transportation, telephone, electric and gas companies, etc. – should be established by public bodies such as the Canadian Transport Commission rather than by the utilities themselves, which are usually monopolies and therefore not subject to competition. The question now arises whether other industries that have developed along monopolistic or oligopolistic lines should be subject to some form of public scrutiny of prices. Since the Canadian economy is a relatively open one, the laid-down costs and, in turn, prices of imported commodities serve as a check on domestic prices in many instances. But this does not necessarily hold true in times of shortages when foreign products are not available.

A permanent public body should be established to review proposed price increases in all industries where there is no real competition (industries structured along monopolistic or oligopolistic lines). This is not to say that all price increases should be prohibited. The Canadian Transport Commission for example, in dealing with railway or telephone rates, handles each case as it arises. Nor do I suggest that the proposed enforcing body should be instructed to deal with proposed price increases in detail. In the automobile industry, for example, such a body might approve a general over-all price increase of, perhaps, five per cent. It would be up to the various companies in the industry to apply the average over-all rate to their various models.

In examining the structure of Canadian industry, one should also consider the distribution of the labour force. The figures shown in Tables 8 and 9 are based on averages for 1974.

Table 8
EMPLOYMENT BY INDUSTRY
000's

Agriculture	473
Other primary	234
Manufacturing	2,024
Construction	598
Transportation, Communication and other utilities	790
Trade	1,575
Finance, Insurance and Real Estate	446
Community, Business and Personal Services	2,386
Public Administration	613
Total	9,137

Table 9
EMPLOYMENT BY REGIONS
000's

Atlantic provinces	701
Quebec	2,427
Ontario	3,519
Prairie provinces	1,494
British Columbia	996
Total	9,137

Slightly more than two million people are employed in manufacturing. The majority of these are employed in manufacturing establishments in Ontario and Quebec. More than half a million of them work in manufacturing plants in other provinces. All these other provinces would like to have more manufacturing done within their borders. This will probably occur as their populations grow.

Despite these facts, a senior government official, who should have known better, argued not so very long ago that in future more and more Canadians would find employment in the resource and service industries; secondary manufacturing, which he believed was relatively inefficient, would become less and less important. He seemed to favour free trade or a common market with the United States.* On the latter point, I suppose there may be room for some differences of opinion respecting the material advantages or disadvantages. There is no room for argument if one wishes Canada to retain her independence as a separate sovereign state.

It is true as is often said that Canada is something of an economic anachronism – but so are many other countries. It is true also that our present system, with its emphasis on east-west rather than north-south communications, may seem costly and illogical. But while economic integration with the United States might result eventually in some very slight marginal reduction in average living costs for all the people of North America, especially those living south of the present border, it could have very serious economic as well as political effects on Canada. Any study of markets and of North American freight rates suggests the likelihood that, under a free trade arrangement, most new manufacturing plants would be built south of the border. Therefore, many young Canadians seeking work in the manufacturing sector of the economy would have to move to the United States (They might not wish to do this in view of the differences between the ways of life in that country and in Canada.)

*A recent report of the Economic Council of Canada along these lines has since been published.

Those who remained in Canada, including most older people, would have to bear a higher per capita tax load than would otherwise be the case. Moreover, any such scheme for integrating the two economies would result in serious social upheavals and disruptions.

Quite apart from the above considerations and as noted in Chapter 2, the average GNP per capita has been growing more rapidly in Canada than in the United States. In 1974, the difference between the two was less than six per cent. Surely this in itself should silence those who claim that integration with the United States would be beneficial for Canadians.

But the strength of those who advocate a continentalist approach should not be underestimated. They include businessmen whose companies might benefit from such an arrangement – including Americans who direct some of our largest corporations. They include visitors from the United States who would like us to share the same kind of living conditions they do. They include some of the members of the Canadian-American Committee, most of whose funds were provided originally by American corporations and their subsidiaries in Canada. Most importantly, they include many Canadians who teach, or have been taught and still believe in, the validity of neo-classical economic theory as applied to Canada. Some influential members of the civil service fall into this category.

Against these powerful groups with continentalist leanings are ranged the political facts of life in Canada. Canadian politicians are not likely to support proposals many people would interpret as leading to our eventual absorption by the United States. It was this belief – this political fact of life – that defeated Sir Wilfrid Laurier in the reciprocity election of 1911. More recently, in the late 1940's, the Right Honourable William Lyon Mackenzie King engaged in secret negotiations with a view to economic integration with the United States. But Mr. King was a believer in the occult and perhaps talked things over with the shade of Sir Wilfrid. In any event, he dropped the whole idea of integration before word got out that he was thinking about it seriously. He was a wily politician. Government officials should remember these political realities as well as the economic considerations before voicing such proposals.

It is difficult to generalize about the relative efficiency of secondary manufacturing and the service industries respectively. A major component of the latter would include those in government service, many of whom would not rate too high in terms of productivity. While the same could be said of some of those employed in secondary manufacturing, there are other sections of that broad sector whose productivity and low costs permit them to compete successfully throughout the world. It does not follow, therefore, that transferring workers from manufacturing to the service industries would necessarily mean an improvement in living standards. In fact, the exact opposite might be the case. In any event, it would be quite impractical to transfer one or two million workers from manufacturing to other sectors of the economy. Moreover, the service sector is rather passive, depending largely for its expansion on other sectors of the economy. It has been found that manufacturing industries, because they provide more employment, relatively, than most resource industries, make a substantially greater contribution to the growth of the service sector. This is another important factor which should not be ignored.

The secondary manufacturing establishments are for the most part supported by relatively modest tariffs. It is often pointed out that this has the effect of increasing costs throughout the country. Some people believe that all tariffs are inherently contrary to the best interests of Canadians except perhaps of a few rich manufacturers. Undoubtedly, this is true in the case of very high tariffs. It is true also that any tariffs do add to costs. If Canadian consumers could import the goods they need, such as refrigerators or bath tubs, direct from the United States or elsewhere, without payment of customs duties, the costs of such goods to them would be lower. But if, as a result, many of the people employed in secondary manufacturing establishments in Canada were to lose their jobs, there would be other costs to be borne, social as well as economic.

There must be a happy medium. And we should keep things in perspective. It is not always realized, for example, that tariff rates in Canada have been steadily reduced ever since the National Policy of Sir John A. Macdonald was introduced in 1879, with the exception of a short period in the 1930's under R. B. Bennett. The last major reduction took place during the so-called Kennedy Round under the GATT (General Agreement on Tariffs and Trade) in the 1960's. The reductions proposed by Canada at that time were substantial; most rates were reduced over a period of years to not more than twelve and one-half or fifteen per cent, and many of them were cut to ten per cent or lower. The average Canadian tariff on all imports is now six per cent. The average on dutiable imports is fifteen per cent. The rates on some items are higher. For example, the former high rates of duty (thirty-five per cent) on shoes and on certain types of textiles were reduced only to twenty or twenty-five per cent. The reason for maintaining these relatively high rates was that certain communities in Quebec and Ontario were entirely dependent for employment on the boot and shoe and textile plants in their vicinities. If these industries had been put out of business, it would have been necessary to move the inhabitants of some of these small towns and villages to other areas. The economic, political, and social costs of doing so would have been prohibitive.

However, there is room for some further modest reductions in the tariff. In any new international negotiations, we should take a good hard look at all rates in excess of, say, fifteen per cent – always providing that, in such negotiations, other countries are willing to make comparable cuts in their own tariff rates.

But, we should not consider eliminating tariffs completely. Manufacturers and their employees must have a reasonable degree of assurance that their operations will not be interrupted by periodic dumping of foreign goods into Canada at less than their cost of production. Manufacturers can always appeal for help under the antidumping laws. But frequently, by the time complaints are investigated, the dumped goods have been distributed and sold in Canada and the harm is done.

Many academic economists who blame the tariff for Canada's economic difficulties have long advocated a floating exchange rate. The Canadian dollar has now been floating since 1970. To the extent that the rate may be reduced from present levels, a measure of protection would be provided for domestic manufacturers and high tariffs would be unnecessary. A lower exchange rate for the Canadian dollar is preferable to high tariffs, because, quite apart from assisting domestic manufacturers, it would stimulate our exports, including exports of industrial raw materials. In other words, a lower exchange rate would tend to help the economies of all regions of the country – both those that depend on manufacturing and those where the great primary resources industries are of key importance. A lower exchange rate would, however, tend to increase the cost of imported consumer goods and thus increase the cost of living.

Let me add that I suspect that Canadian freight rates may have as much to do with the cost of some consumer products in Eastern and Western Canada as the tariff.

On balance, the best solution for this thorny problem –

given the political facts of life in Canada, the distribution of our working population, and regional disparities – may be to aim for a lower exchange rate for the Canadian dollar; for further modest reductions in, but not complete abolition of, the tariff; and for substantial subsidies to the railroads in exchange for appreciable reductions in freight rates to the West and to the East. This would make more sense than the opinion sometimes expressed that the Canadian economy would flourish much better if we were to eliminate all tariffs.

There has been a lot of talk in the last few years — but I suspect a good deal less hard thinking – about the need for a new industrial strategy for Canada. Some may think the answer lies in phasing out our secondary manufacturing establishments. Others believe that more of our secondary manufacturing industries should be rationalized; that more production should be concentrated in fewer plants. The latter is not likely to take place as long as so many of these plants are controlled by manufacturers in the United States. Anti-trust laws in that country restrain the u.s. owners of plants in Canada or their agents here from even discussing possibilities of mergers.

My own hunch is that Canada will continue to need its great primary industries and will need also a secondary manufacturing sector – preferably distributed throughout the country to a greater extent than is the case at present. It seems highly probable that employment in the service sector of the economy will continue to increase. However, I would hope that increases in the civil service at all levels of government would be held to a minimum and that steps be taken to increase the efficiency in government service generally.

Before closing this discussion on the structure of Canadian industry, I should say something about the importance of our banking system which plays a crucial role in Canadian industry. Canada has an excellent banking system and we can take it for granted that its ten chartered banks, which are under the continuous scrutiny of the Inspector General of Banks, are in sound shape. Five of the ten banks have branches throughout the country and are of a size to compare with the large banks throughout the world. The Banque Canadienne Nationale and the Provinciale Banque du Canada originally were established to serve the Province of Quebec, but are now spreading their operations into other parts of Canada. The Bank of British Columbia is largely confined to that province. The Unity Bank, incorporated in 1972, is only beginning to get under way. The Mercantile Bank, controlled by National City Bank of New York (Citibank), is the only foreign-controlled commercial bank in Canada. As was to be expected, it is growing fast. It does much of its business with Canadian subsidiaries of u.s. clients of Citibank. Because Citibank has now reduced its holdings to twenty-five per cent of the shares of Mercantile, Mercantile is now hailed as being controlled in Canada. This, of course, is nonsense. Citibank's twenty-five per cent gives it effective control of Mercantile. In the case of all other banks, no more than a total of twenty-five per cent of their shares may be held by foreigners and no more than ten per cent by any single foreigner or associated group. The same rule should apply in the case of Mercantile.

The ten chartered banks are not the only institutions that accept deposits in Canada. The first thing that strikes one from a perusal of Table 10 is the tremendous increase in the volume of deposits that has occurred in the last ten years. This reflects the increase in economic activity during the same period. Secondly, few changes have occurred in the relative positions of the various institutions. Trust companies have gained ground it is true, but nothing has happened to detract from the pre-eminent place of the chartered banks.

Table 10
TOTAL DEPOSITS OR DEPOSIT-TYPE LIABILITIES AT END OF 1964 AND 1974

	1964		1974	
	Amount (in billions)	Percentage of total	Amount (in billions)	Percentage of total
Chartered Banks:				
The 3 largest (Royal, Commerce, Montreal)	$11.6	49%	$40.9	50%
The 7 others (Nova Scotia, Toronto Dominion, Nationale, Provinciale, Mercantile, B.C., Unity)	5.1	21	17.9	21
Total	16.7	70	58.8	71
Trust Companies	2.5	10	11.1	14
Credit Unions and Caisses Populaires	1.9	8	7.0	9
Mortgage Loan Companies	1.3	5	4.6	5
Quebec Savings Banks	0.4	2	0.9	1
All others	1.1	5	n.a.	n.a.
	$23.9	100%	$82.4	100%

The banking business in Canada is structured along oligopolistic lines. Its growth is dependent on the growth of the money supply and therefore on periodic decisions of the federal government acting through the Bank of Canada. For these reasons, and because of their great importance to the national economy, the operations of the chartered banks are subject to supervision by government agencies.

From the time of Confederation until the 1967 amendments to the Bank Act, limits were placed on the rates of interest the chartered banks were allowed to charge their customers. The Royal Commission on Banking and Finance (the Porter Commission), 1961 to 1964, recommended that such restrictions be removed and argued that under a free competitive system rates would be reduced. This strange belief was shared by the Minister of Finance in 1967, who, despite the scepticism of many MP's respecting the altruism of bankers, succeeded in persuading Parliament to remove the interest rate ceiling of six per cent. As was predicted, the rates were increased immediately.

This is not to say that a fixed ceiling of six per cent could or should have been maintained. If world interest rates were to keep on rising, as they did do, provision would have been needed to permit some flexibility in the rates charged by the Canadian chartered banks. But such provision should have included safeguards against the public being overcharged by what is essentially an oligopolistic industry.

One suggestion put forward somewhat tentatively in 1966 was to tie the prime rate chargeable by the chartered banks to the "Bank Rate" announced from time to time by the Bank of Canada. This, or some other appropriate formula, might be worth reconsidering when the Bank Act is next up for review in 1977.

Despite the prohibitions of the revised Bank Act, many foreign banking institutions have opened offices in Canada recently. They have done so under the authority of provincial charters, often with little or no capital.

In a speech on April 18th, 1975, Mr. Richard M. Thomson, President of The Toronto Dominion Bank, stated there are some 170 of these Canadian subsidiaries of foreign banks operating in Canada that are not subject to supervision by the federal authorities. He added that lack of such regulations poses a threat to the stability of the Canadian money market.

I agree with Mr. Thomson. The subsidiaries of foreign banks that have come to Canada by the back door, so to speak, should be subjected to all the supervision and other conditions of the Bank Act, including the requirements respecting ownership that apply to the regularly constituted chartered banks.

Chapter 4.

Policies for Economic Stability

John Maynard Keynes' theories for stimulating or slowing down the economy were promulgated during the Great Depression of the 1930's. While *The General Theory of Employment, Interest and Money*, published in 1936, was not exactly easy reading for the layman, it revolutionized the economic thinking of succeeding generations. Keynes' advocacy of expansive fiscal and monetary policies during periods of recession or depression has been generally accepted. But his contrary advice of reduced government expenditures and higher taxes to slow down the economy in boom periods in order to contain inflation has been more difficult for democratic governments to apply. When times are bad, few voters oppose programs to increase government expenditures and reduce taxes. They are less enthusiastic, however, when the times call for reduced expenditures and higher taxes.

Take a Canadian example. In the fall of 1969, the government decided to slow down the economy in order to dampen inflationary pressures which were apparent at the time. A variety of measures were approved with this as the objective, measures that were not popular with the voters. Among other things, they resulted in a lower rate of economic activity and increased unemployment that proved difficult to reverse. There were those who warned the government at the time that it was easy enough to slow down the economy, but it would be much harder and would take a good deal longer to get it moving ahead again. This proved to be the case. As a consequence, the government was almost defeated in the next general election held on October 30, 1972. Trudeau's Liberals won one hundred and nine seats, a loss of thirty-eight. Stanfield's Conservatives won one hundred and seven seats and the NDP, thirty-one. Trudeau managed to hang onto power by his eyelashes, but for the next eighteen months his minority government lived a precarious existence. This political lesson is not likely to be forgotten the next time a Canadian government is urged to embark upon an extended austerity program.

But quite apart from the question of restrictive measures being unpopular with the voters, the Keynesian proposals for economic stability in the short term had two specific requirements that frequently were not met in the postwar period. First, they required a good system of forecasting, to anticipate the turning points in the economy, the beginnings of recessions and recoveries, with a reasonable degree of accuracy. Secondly, they assumed that governments and parliaments would be able to act promptly and that they would develop programs that could be initiated and interrupted quickly.

The business cycle, with its phases of recession, recovery and boom, is a relatively regular phenomenon lasting between three and four years. But Canadian governments have not always been right in their assessment of the position of the cycle and therefore of the kind of policies needed to stimulate recovery or to restrain a boom. Let me cite a few examples of governments guessing wrongly and, as a consequence, approving policies of stimulation or restraint at the wrong times and thus aggravating the situations they hoped to ameliorate.

The first real postwar recession began at the end of

1953 but the government of the day did not begin to counteract it until it produced its budget in 1955. Its provisions contributed to exaggerating the boom of 1956. Another downward movement started early in 1957 but a new government was elected in June of that year. Its measures for countering the downturn were understandably delayed and, when they did come, may have been influenced more by the political pressures of a new election than by counter-cyclical budgetting. Whatever the reasons, the budget deficit for the fiscal year 1958-59 was late, insofar as the business cycle was concerned. As another example, the government announced an austerity program in September 1966 just at the beginning of a pause in economic activity and abandoned those measures in 1967 when the pause was over. Early in 1970, when in fact another recession had begun, the Budget delivered in March contained further measures, including control of consumer credit, to reduce total demand.

According to an announcement made by the U.S. Department of Commerce in April of 1975, the recent recession in the United States began in November 1973. Yet President Nixon stated in January 1974 that there would be no recession. In September, President Ford made a similar assertion, insisting that inflation was the major immediate problem, and he proposed to increase taxes. He changed his views some three months later. The U.S. Congress approved its own version of tax cuts in March 1975, a year and a half after the recession had begun. The U.S. budget deficit for the fiscal year commencing July 1 will exceed $70 billion and will have its full impact on the aggregate demand for funds and the structure of interest rates precisely at a time when most forecasters seem to agree that the U.S. economy will be well on the road to recovery.

In Canada, recent government performance has not been very much better. The GNP in constant dollars ceased to grow at the end of the first quarter of 1974, and accordingly measures to stimulate the economy were in order. However, the "Bank Rate" determined by the Bank of Canada was raised a full percentage point to eight and one-quarter per cent on April 15 of that year, to eight and three-quarter per cent on May 13, and to nine and one-quarter per cent on July 24. It remained at that level until November 18 when it was reduced to eight and three-quarter per cent. Thus, throughout the first stages of the recession, we had a restrictive monetary policy which, among other things, discouraged housing construction. The November budget recognized the slowdown but its main tax proposals were not approved by Parliament until the end of March 1975.

Thus, on the whole, governments have tended to try to counter cyclical inflation and recession when it was too late and, in the process, have contributed to increased prices and to unemployment. This lack of precision should be corrected. Otherwise we shall run the risk of planting the seeds for another recession in late 1977 or early 1978.

When the times call for stimulating the economy – as they still do, to a moderate extent, in Canada at the time of writing – there are many things a government can do. The first obvious move is to reduce taxes to stimulate consumer spending. The government has already done this. The emphasis should be on reductions in regressive taxes such as sales taxes. Reductions in personal income taxes tend to benefit the rich more than the poor and have less influence on consumer spending. Secondly, the government can increase its capital expenditures. However, these usually take a considerable time to plan and implement and are hard to shut off again when the times call for restraint.

Under present conditions, the government no doubt is considering ways and means to stimulate the housing industry. I would hope this will include substantial subsidies, such as greatly reduced rates of interest on mortgages, to first buyers of new houses. Apart from stimulating the economy, the objective should be to make housing available for newly established families at costs they can afford.*

Other measures for stimulating the economy include an easy money policy; reduced interest rates; and concerted moves to reduce the value of the Canadian dollar. The exchange rate for the Canadian dollar was falling during mid-1975 and will probably continue to do so in light of the tremendous deficit in our transactions with other countries that we face. I would hope the government authorities do not get panicky and try to stem this trend. On the contrary, they should encourage a fall in the value of the Canadian dollar in all ways open to them. A significant reduction in the value of the dollar would stimulate both our resource and manufacturing industries and thus help to reduce the very high levels of unemployment – but admittedly at the price of some rise in the cost of living.

Canada is still in a period of recession (perhaps about at the end of the downturn at the time of writing) with very heavy unemployment and inflation. In these circumstances, the thrust of government policies should be to stimulate the economy for a while longer rather than to concentrate on inflation. In a few years' time, however, inflation may well become our major problem once again. For this reason, I propose to devote a good part of this chapter to a discussion of it. Inflation of the kind and severity we have suffered from in the past two years or so must be taken with the utmost seriousness. It bears most heavily on people with fixed incomes and on those at the lower levels of the income scale. It erodes and destroys confidence in our social system. New Canadians who remember what happened in Europe after World War I especially fear it. It is a disease that everyone in authority must do his utmost to contain.

Historically, wars – which are paid for in part by major

* This was written in early May 1975. Little stimulus to housing was in fact provided in the mid-summer budget.

increases in the money supply – are accompanied or followed by inflation. This often spreads to other countries that were not directly involved in the hostilities. There was extreme inflation in Europe after World War I. In some countries, the values of the currencies were wiped out completely. There was serious inflation in Canada also from 1917 to 1921. Again, following World War II, there was such severe pressure on prices in Canada that the whole machinery of the Wartime Prices and Trade Board had to be hastily dismantled, and prices rose sharply. There were similar price rises after the Korean War in 1951. It is not surprising, therefore, that the Western World should be suffering another serious bout of inflation following the end of the disastrous war in Vietnam. This time the situation has been aggravated by world shortages of oil and the very considerable price increases imposed by the oil producing countries; by food shortages caused by climatic conditions; and the price increases imposed by other commodity producers. It has been aggravated also by the exponential rates of growth of all the industrialized countries (especially the United States) and their ever-expanding consumption of non-renewable resources. Some of these conditions were exceptional and should not repeat themselves. There is no doubt, however, that "cost push" inflation, because of the exercise of private monopolistic controls on the supply side, has become chronic and one of the most dangerous structural problems of our economic system.

Perhaps partly because of its near defeat in the October 1972 election, the government has been hesitant about introducing effective anti-inflationary measures. There was a good deal of talk about inflation as a world-wide phenomenon; about the helplessness of individual countries to do very much about it. Later, the Minister of Finance advocated a policy of voluntary restraints, but this did not appeal very much to organized labour and has been pretty well abandoned. It is true that inflation has been and is world-wide in scope and no one should claim that Canada by itself can avoid its ravagès. But it is not true that Canada is helpless. There are things that could have been done and still could be done to reduce considerably, if not eliminate entirely, the effects of inflation in this country. These do not include a restrictive monetary policy which, as I shall argue later can do more harm than good in a widely diverse country like Canada.

An effective way of restraining inflation in Canada would include a mix or a variety of measures. In a long and perceptive article in the Insight Section of *The Toronto Star* on February 1, 1975, William A. Dimma, Dean of the Faculty of Administrative Studies at York University, argued for temporary wage and price controls. In doing so, he pointed out one of the main arguments against this: "It has been said that wage-and-price controls have never worked in a democracy in peacetime and will not work now. Certainly, they will not work unless a majority of Canadians want them to work. That condition will not be met until wage-and-price controls are perceived by most reasonable persons as preferable to the alternatives. At the moment the alternatives are an accelerating inflation or sterner monetary and fiscal measures than yet taken. Either carries a serious risk of eventual economic collapse."

It was suggested in Chapter 3 that some form of permanent public authority should be established to control price increases in industries structured along monopolistic or oligopolistic lines. The responsibilities of such an authority could be extended temporarily to other key commodities and services in periods of serious inflation and should apply to such things as rents, certain industrial materials and such es-

sential consumer items as clothing, shoes, etc. The controls
on consumer items should be applied at the manufacturers'
level with restrictions on the amount of mark-up that retailers
would be allowed to add. It can be argued that any degree of
inflation is serious; but I have in mind periods in which inflation rates are rising and have reached levels of about five per
cent per annum. I would not be inclined to include conditions
when inflation rates, while much higher than five per cent,
appear to be on a downward trend – if this trend is expected
to continue.*

In periods of serious inflation, the Food Prices Review
Board could be given authority over the prices of basic
foodstuffs. And the Bank of Canada or the Inspector
General of Banks could be authorized to control interest
rates and to restrain the chartered banks from making certain
types of loans, including restrictions on consumer credit,
either or directly or indirectly through the acceptance companies.

Businessmen will argue that, if there is to be any type of
price controls, there should also be wage controls; that one
without the other would be manifestly unfair. Organized
labour, for its part, has been opposed to an
incomes policy in any form and from time to time in the
past has been able to demonstrate that wage rates have
lagged behind increases in prices and the cost of living.
While this is no longer true, it seems unlikely at present
that labour leaders would accept *voluntarily* an incomes
policy including enforceable wage controls. Nor are most
of them ready to give up *voluntarily* the right to strike as
their ultimate weapon in favour of some form of compul-

* This was written in early May, 1975. Subsequent increases in oil
  and gas prices, the tax on gasoline imposed in the mid-summer
  budget and the increase in Bank Rate announced on September
  2nd, will slow the anticipated reduction in the rate of inflation quite
  considerably if not stop it altogether.

sory arbitration. And yet if there is no restraint on both prices and wages, we shall have serious inflation once again, which eventually may well lead to a depression.

Moreover, if prices and wages continue to increase, our export goods may be priced out of world markets. Examples can be cited of wage rates that are considerably higher in Canada than in comparable operations in the United States despite lower productivity here. This should serve as a serious warning of trouble ahead.

In periods of rising inflation, some government authority should indicate the kind of wage increases in various industries that it would consider fair and reasonable in settling wage contracts in the coming months. (For the program to be successful, the proposed wage increases should be on the generous side.) This should place some restraint on excessive demands by organized labour. Moreover, coupled with the kind of price controls suggested, it would also place some restraint on what increased wages businessmen could agree to if the full amount of any increases could no longer be passed on more or less automatically to consumers.

To be successful, an approach along these lines would need the cooperation and support of trade union leaders, but, if at all possible, I would like to see it tried before resorting to a program of full-scale wage and price controls.

This may be as good a place as any to refer to labour's right to strike in such essential services as police and fire protection, hospital staffs, the basic transportation and postal services, and perhaps as well in other government services. Unless and until some alternative guarantees of a fair method of settling disputes can be devised, labour is unlikely to accede this right. If the government and the labour movement were able to produce a formula acceptable to both – one which would protect labour from the effects of inflation and include a share in any increases from productivity – it would be a welcome move for all concerned including, in particular, members of the general public. If this objective proved to be impossible – and if the public continues to be inconvenienced at a time of recession, much too high levels of unemployment, and still rising prices – then Parliament and the Provincial Legislatures should legislate against further strikes in the essential and public services. If the right to strike should be withdrawn, the position of public servants might be protected by making their salaries and wages adjustable with changes in the composite index of wages and salaries in the private sector. In any event, it would be important to take a sympathetic and understanding view of labour's legitimate interests – as well as those of the general public – and to provide for procedures of arbitration that will make this clear to all concerned.

If and when it becomes necessary to take the kind of measures suggested for restraining serious rates of inflation once again, let us hope our elected leaders will give a better example to the general public. If Members of Parliament give the impression they are out for all they can get for themselves, as they did at the end of last year in asking for a fifty per cent increase in their remuneration, it will be difficult to persuade others to be less greedy.

I have not advocated the use of the traditional tight money policy as a counter to inflation. A restrictive monetary policy designed to slow down business activity is a very blunt instrument indeed for restraining inflation in a country like Canada, because of the way its effects are felt unevenly throughout the country. Such a policy may be called for in, say, Ontario and the Western provinces at a time when the economies of those regions are overheated. But conditions may be very different in the Atlantic area and in Eastern Quebec where unacceptable levels of unemployment may prevail. A restrictive monetary policy would inevitably exacerbate the situation in these areas. It has done so in the past, and frequently the impersonal and invisible central bankers in Ottawa have been blamed. This, of course, is not quite fair. Since the Bank of Canada Act was amended in 1967, the government, not the Bank, has been responsible for monetary policy and thus for aggravating unemployment conditions in Eastern Canada when such policy is restrictive.

Moreover, foreign-controlled companies in Canada can more frequently avoid the restraining influences of a restrictive monetary policy than can their Canadian-controlled competitors. If necessary, the former can borrow funds for expansion or for operating purposes from their foreign parents.

Parliament has passed legislation incorporating the Business Development Bank, responsible to the Minister of Industry, Trade and Commerce. The new bank (with a capitalization of $125 million) will take over the Industrial Development Bank (formerly a subsidiary of the Bank of Canada). It is to be hoped the reorganized Bank will be operated in such a way as to provide a degree of flexibility in monetary policy. For example, if conditions call for a measure of restraint in, say, Ontario and a degree of stimulation in Eastern Canada, the managers of the Business Development Bank could be instructed to be very tough in their loans policy in Ontario and very easy in Eastern Canada. This would be a new philosophy for bankers but a not inappropriate one given regional disparities in Canada.

Admittedly, a policy along these lines by the Business Development Bank could have only a marginal effect in smoothing the impact in some areas of a restrictive monetary policy. The possibilities of developing techniques for applying monetary policy on a regional basis that would have a greater and more general impact should be the subject of further thought.

A major inflationary factor in the recent rising costs of many goods and services (for example, rents and housing) has been high, usurious rates of interest. Interest rates nearly doubled between 1973 and 1974, and, as was to be expected, so did the cost of housing – an important factor in the cost of living. Obviously, if world-wide interest rates are very high, especially in the United States, they will be high in Canada. But in the last few years, they have been higher here than necessary. Historically, the Bank of Canada has kept long-term interest rates at not less than about one and a half per cent above the rates prevailing in the United States. This practice stemmed from the days when Canada had a fixed exchange rate and was running large deficits on current account in its balance of payments. These deficits were balanced by inflows of capital encouraged by the higher interest rates in Canada. Now, with a floating exchange rate, we could have a smaller differential in interest rates with the United States than has hitherto prevailed. If this resulted in some outflow of funds from Canada, and thus in a further reduction in the value of the Canadian dollar in terms of the u.s. dollar, so much the better.

Chapter 5.

Energy Policy

Until the fall of 1974, most Canadians believed we had more or less unlimited reserves of oil and gas. Back in 1970, the then Minister of Energy, Mines and Resources asserted that Canada's oil reserves (he meant developed and potential reserves) were sufficient for our needs for more than nine hundred years and our natural gas reserves would be good for nearly four hundred years. This feeling of extreme confidence about Canada's reserves or readily established reserves was shared by spokesmen for the oil industry itself – an industry dominated by the Canadian subsidiaries of the international oil companies. The most important company is Imperial Oil, 70 per cent owned by the Exxon Corporation of New York. The next largest companies are Gulf Canada, 68.3 per cent owned by Gulf Corporation, U.S.A.; Shell Canada, controlled by Royal Dutch – Shell, which in turn is 40 per cent British, 21 per cent U.S. and 19 per cent Dutch; and Texaco Canada Limited, 68.2 per cent owned by Texaco Inc., U.S.A.

It is significant that during the period of over-optimism and complacency, when government officials seemed to be in general agreement with the estimates and the views of the oil companies, a number of independent Canadians, with no personal axes to grind began to ask some searching questions. I should like to mention some of them.

Dean R. St. J. Macdonald and Professors Douglas M. Johnston, Rowland J. H. Harrison, and Ian McDougall of Dalhousie University prepared a brief, "Economic Development with Environmental Security," towards the end of 1972 that posed some serious questions. Professor F. K. North, the Carleton University geologist, has continually raised questions about the conventional wisdom of the day respecting the amount of our reserves. Bruce Willson, an Alberta gas man and later President of the Union Gas Company; Mel Hurtig and Jim Ryan of Edmonton; the Honourable Eric Kierans; Professor Tuzo Wilson, the internationally known geophysicist; Professor John Helliwell of Vancouver; Kit Vincent of the Canadian Arctic Resources Committee; Professor Robert Page of the Committee for an Independent Canada, who recently has written an informative article on the National Energy Board; and Professor Edgar Dosman of York University, whose book is to be published in the fall of this year, are others who have been prepared to voice their concerns about what has been going on. Hurtig, in his role of publisher, commissioned Philip Sykes to write *Sellout, the Giveaway of Canada's Energy Resources*, published in 1973. Richard Rohmer's book *The Arctic Imperative* was published in the same year. Early in 1974, Professor James Laxer, also of York University, wrote another book, *Canada's Energy Crisis*, which at the time of writing, is about to be reprinted with a new concluding chapter. David Crane of *The Toronto Star* has written some first-class articles on the subject over a period of several years. His most recent series, to be published in the fall of 1975, is a serious indictment of the way things have been misjudged and mishandled.

Others like myself, with no direct connections with the oil industry, began asking questions a few years ago. In the course of a speech at McMaster University in February 1973, I posed a number of questions about the proposed Mackenzie River Valley gas pipe line and the oil industry in general. I went on to say

> There is another fundamental question of principle which should be settled before we proceed much farther. Should Canada's reserves of oil and natural gas – and especially her potential reserves in the North including the Arctic Islands, which come under federal jurisdiction – be considered a highly important national asset in which all Canadians have a vital stake? Or should these potential reserves or some part of them be allowed to be acquired and exploited by a relatively few, but very powerful and no doubt very efficient, U.S. and other foreign oil companies through their subsidiaries in Canada?

I raised this again in Calgary, in June 1973, during a debate with a representative of the oil industry, Charles Hetherington, the head of Panarctic Oils. Mr. Hetherington strongly favoured a "free enterprise" approach to oil and gas development. Considering his company is forty-five per cent owned by the federal government, this view seemed a bit ironical! In stating the contrary opinion, I said: "I believe in free enterprise as a general rule, particularly if it means a considerable degree of decentralization of the decision-making process. But I do not agree with the concept if it means that control is exercised by foreigners, especially in the case of an industry that is oligopolistic in its structure, as is the oil industry. In such situations, one may ask – free enterprise for whom and in whose best interests?"

Many public spirited Canadians, who should not be dismissed as cranks and radicals, have questioned whether the Canadian oil industry, dominated as it is by the subsidiaries of the international corporations, is being operated in the best interests of Canadians. They have questioned whether the estimates and the propaganda of the Canadian oil industry can be relied upon; and even whether Canadian Government officials have been too easily persuaded by the views of the spokesmen for these giant corporations.

In fairness to everyone concerned – ministers, officials, and oil company spokesmen – it should be recognized that estimating reserves and potential reserves of oil and gas cannot be done with any exactness. This is particularly true of the potential reserves in the Arctic and the Arctic Islands, in which case "guesses" might be a better word to use than estimates. Nor can estimates of the costs of exploration and development, or the costs and availability of transportation facilities for such reserves, be calculated with any precision (quite apart from the question of inflation). These reservations should be kept in mind when considering the conclusions to be drawn from a welter of industry pronouncements, government assertions, and conflicting accusations during the last few years. I shall try to deal with these in summary fashion going back about five years. In doing so, in the case of oil, I shall draw on a long article by David Crane, published in *The Toronto Star* at the beginning of 1975.

In 1969, the National Energy Board, (NEB) published a very optimistic report. The Board indicated that the amount of oil Canada could produce in the next twenty years would depend, not on the supplies available, but primarily upon the level of imports permitted by the U.S. and upon a decision by the Canadian Government on whether Quebec and the Atlantic provinces would switch from imported to Canadian oil.

The Canadian Government pressed the United States to allow greater imports of oil and gas; we were irritated when the U.S. authorities imposed quotas or other restrictions on our petroleum exports.

Early in 1973, a new study was published which, while

warning of possible limitations to Canadian supplies in the 1980's, was optimistic about supplies for the longer term. It forecast that, by 1980, Mackenzie Delta oil would be on stream, and that significant amounts of oil sand and heavy oils would be available. This state of optimism respecting Canada's oil reserves continued until the fall of 1974.

In the meantime, in October 1973, the Organization of Petroleum Exporting Countries (OPEC) increased substantially the international price of oil exports from $3 a barrel with a further increase shortly afterwards to $11 a barrel. This put the cat among the pigeons and produced an international crisis of very grave proportions.

In the fall of 1973, following the price increases by OPEC, the Canadian Government established a two-price system for Canadian oil – a fixed domestic price and an export price that moved upward with the going international price. This initiative, while popular with Canadian consumers, was bitterly opposed by the oil industry and by the government of Alberta. It was a courageous decision by the Honourable Donald S. Macdonald, the Minister of Energy, Mines and Resources, and the minority government of the day. It was a bit ironic that the move to hold down the price of oil for Canadians was not supported by the Progressive Conservatives in Ottawa, perhaps in deference to the views of the Conservative government in Alberta, or by the New Democratic Party (NDP), possibly in deference to their political friends in Saskatchewan.

The lower price of fuel in Canada gave an appreciable advantage to Canadian industry *vis-a-vis* industry in the U.S. and other countries, who were now forced to pay the world price. In addition, it helped to keep down the cost of living at a time when inflationary pressures were rising ominously.

The oil companies objected to the two-price system and are still doing so. They claim that higher prices are needed as an incentive to further exploration. It was about this time that they began to scale down very considerably their previous estimates of reserves.

This campaign proved effective. In the spring of 1974, the government approved an increase in the price of Canadian crude oil from $4.00 to $6.50 a barrel. Although the government retained the two-price system, it was a victory for the oil companies, for the Alberta Government, and for the U.S. Government. It was a victory for the U.S. Government because the difference between U.S. and Canadian prices was reduced, and the export tax that the U.S. had strenuously opposed was reduced proportionately.

About this time, Marshall Crowe, an economist, a former Deputy Secretary of the Cabinet, and at the time Chairman of the Canada Development Corporation, was appointed to succeed Robert D. Howland as Chairman of the National Energy Board.

In the May 1974 budget, oil royalties charged by provincial governments were disallowed as deductions from taxable income. This was an attempt by the Minister of Finance, the Honourable John Turner, to secure some part of the increased profits of the oil companies for the federal government in the form of taxes. As was to be expected, it provoked howls of anguish from the oil companies and the governments of Alberta and Saskatchewan. In Ottawa, the Progressive Conservatives and the NDP voted against the budget (for a variety of reasons) and the Liberal government was defeated to be re-elected with an over-all majority on October 30, 1974.

The NEB held a series of hearings in April and May, 1974 on the question of Canadian oil reserves and quantities available for export. Following these hearings, the board's report in October of 1974 reversed its own previous forecasts. It concluded that the demand for Canadian crude oil would exceed supply by 1982. No longer was there any thought of Mackenzie Delta oil becoming available for at least ten years. Gone, too, was the previous optimism about the tar sands.

On the basis of its new estimates, the NEB recommended the gradual scaling down of oil exports to the U.S. from 1975 until 1982, the year when Canadian demand was expected to exceed supply, at which time exports should be discontinued altogether.

However, the report of the NEB was not entirely pessimistic. Despite its sharply reduced estimates of reserves, the board expressed its ultimate faith in Canada's potential provided the price is right: " . . . given sufficient lead time and proper economic incentives, there is a good prospect that Canada could become self-sufficient in energy for a long period."

In his revised budget of November 1974, the Minister of Finance retained the previous provision of disallowing royalties as an expense for tax purposes, but made some quite substantial concessions to the oil companies. This did not satisfy them however. With the issue of the NEB report on greatly reduced estimates, the Economic Council of Canada concurrently issued a report in the fall of 1974 recommending the discontinuance of the two-price oil system. At the same time, the Council, with its well-known continentalist leanings, indicated that foreign investment inflows should be doubled between 1974 and the early 1980's.

Despite the fact that the October 1974 NEB report predicted a short fall in domestic oil supplies for eleven years, from 1982 to 1993, the Minister of Energy, Mines and Resources stated in the House of Commons on February 7, 1975, that he expected Canada would have an oil surplus again as early as 1985. The estimates seemed to be going up and down and up again in yo-yo fashion.

In the meantime and consonant with the new reduced

estimates of reserves, the oil companies stepped up their campaign against the two-price system (their campaign for an increase in oil prices) arguing that if they were unable to increase their revenues, they would not be able to do the amount of exploration and development work clearly called for in the light of the new and drastically reduced estimates of reserves. Their campaign had its effect, so much so that at a federal-provincial conference in April 1975, the federal government joined the Alberta Government in supporting an increase in the price of oil. This at a time when the federal government was seriously concerned about inflation, and the Minister of Finance was urging business and labour to accept a program of voluntary restraints. However, largely due to the opposition of Premier Davis of Ontario to any increase in oil prices (with an election in the offing), the conference broke up without agreement.

Current rumour holds that in the near future the federal government will approve unilaterally an increase in the domestic price from $6.50 to $8.50 a barrel and a further increase perhaps to the world price of $11 a barrel possibly in 1976 or 1977.*

According to James Laxer, such price increases would mean that on Alberta's present proven reserves of about six billion barrels, the oil companies will get an additional $12 billion (after taxes and royalties) over the life of the reserves. This estimate is based on the assumption that the present conflict over royalties and income taxes would be resolved to give the oil companies a net increase of about $2 a barrel. If this should happen, it would be quite a windfall profit for the oil companies.

* In the mid-summer budget of 1975 the price was in fact increased by $1.50 a barrel, against the strong resistance of the Ontario Government. A substantial increase in the price of natural gas was subsequently approved.

Table 11
FINANCIAL RESULTS OF THE THREE LARGEST OIL
COMPANIES, 1970 TO 1974

IMPERIAL OIL
(MILLIONS OF DOLLARS)

	Gross Operating Income (Sales)	Net Income	Shareholders' Equity at beginning of year	Rate of Return
1970	$1,680	$105	$ 933	11%
1971	1,907	136	971	14
1972	2,045	151	1,038	14
1973	2,580	228	1,119	20
1974	3,713	(a) 290	1,304	22
Increase in four years from 1970 to 1974	121%	176%	40%	

(a) This includes investment income.

GULF CANADA
(MILLIONS OF DOLLARS)

	Sales	Net Income	Shareholders' Equity at beginning of year	Rate of Return
1970	$ 823	$ 39	$660	6%
1971	934	54	674	8
1972	1,023	64	704	8
1973	1,232	101	742	14
1974	1,476	161	812	20
Increase in four years from 1970 to 1974	79%	313%	23%	

Table 11 Continued

SHELL CANADA

(MILLIONS OF DOLLARS)

	Sales	Net Income	Shareholders Equity at beginning of year	Rate of Return
1970	$ 729	$ 51	$676	7%
1971	788	61	710	8
1972	867	78	756	10
1973	1,077	112	812	14
1974	(a) 1,623	142	896	16
Increase in four years from 1970 to 1974	122%	178%	33%	

(a) Total revenue.

An examination of the financial results of the principal oil companies in Canada shows that the net income of the three largest has increased by 176 per cent, 313 per cent, and 178 per cent respectively in the past four years. In the same period, their rate of return on shareholders' equity increased to 22 per cent, 20 per cent, and 16 per cent, respectively. These figures are significant, although examples could be cited of other companies in other industries that have done even better. But given the oligopolistic nature of the industry, it is difficult to conclude that the major oil companies are entitled to higher prices and, therefore, presumably to even higher profits in the future. Imperial Oil, Gulf Canada and Shell Canada are subsidiaries of global corporations, two of them based in the United States. It can be argued that these three international companies will concentrate their efforts on exploration and development in those parts of the world where they, or their subsidiaries, can make the most money. If this is not the case in Canada, they can always do their exploration and development work somewhere else. This may be true, but I doubt if it is an argument that will prove palatable or convincing to Canadians.

I should say something, rather briefly, about the Alberta tar sands and the Syncrude project. When Premier Lougheed came to power in Alberta, he commissioned a report from Walter J. Levy, the well-known oil consultant, on the development of the oil sands. Mr. Levy urged the government to proceed with the development and in September 1973, the government of Alberta entered into an agreement with Syncrude Canada Limited, a joint venture by Imperial, Gulf, Cities Service, and Atlantic Richfield. A year later, the partners revised upwards very considerably their cost estimates of the project and Atlantic Richfield dropped out. To keep the project alive, the federal, Alberta, and Ontario governments agreed, early in 1975, to invest $600 million in Syncrude for which they obtained a thirty per cent interest.

In addition, the federal government agreed to allow provincial royalty payments as a deduction from taxable income in the case of Syncrude and to permit Syncrude to charge the world price for its product, which is expected to come on stream in 1979. The first of these concessions means the federal government has retreated from its previous position respecting royalties; the second means it is retreating from its position respecting the two-price system for oil. With these two major concessions, it would seem the oil companies are about to win their propaganda battle.

In 1970, the NEB received an application for the export of some nine trillion cubic feet of gas to the United States. It was submitted that reserves were quite sufficient to justify such exports. The NEB approval for the export of 6.3 trillion cubic feet was severely criticized as unwise by some observers. The industry, too, was critical of the board for not approving the export of the full nine trillion cubic feet it had asked for.

In 1973, the Department of Energy, Mines and Resources estimated that Canada had proven reserves of natural gas for twenty-three years at 1972 production levels. It also predicted a further fifteen years' supply as probably available, if still unproven, in the prairies on the same basis. Such optimistic estimates implied that there was no problem insofar as natural gas commitments were concerned, at least for a long time to come. In March 1973, the NEB was saying that Canada had ample reserves to cover requirements to the end of the eighties or the early nineties. A little over a year later, Marshall Crowe, the new chairman of the Board, stated, "It is now evident that shortages of gas supply will appear before the end of the decade." This means within the next five years.

This new and pessimistic estimate bolstered the position of Canadian Arctic Gas Study Ltd., a consortium of companies including Imperial Oil, Gulf Canada, Shell Canada, and many other oil and investment companies, that wishes to build a gas pipe line up the Mackenzie River Valley. They hope this will bring Alaska gas and gas from the Canadian Arctic to Alberta and to the U.S. border. The project is to be studied carefully by a Commission of Inquiry under Mr. Justice Thomas Berger who began hearings on March 4, 1975. Beginning in July of 1975, it is to be studied also by the National Energy Board.

A rival group headed by Alberta Gas Trunk Lines, in opposition to Canadian Arctic Gas Study, wishes to build a somewhat smaller pipe line up the Mackenzie to ship only Canadian gas to Alberta. Others believe that a railway from Hay River, on Great Slave Lake, to the Arctic would be preferable to a pipe line. There seems no disposition to study the possible advantages of this alternative.

If it had not been for the feeling of urgency created by the new and pessimistic estimates of gas reserves announced in May 1974, these enquiries presumably would have been allowed to take their natural courses and the necessary time taken to consider the various alternatives. They would also have had time to consider carefully the rights of the native peoples and important questions relating to the ecology of the region. However, it has been alleged, and not denied, that some members of the Cabinet have already come down in favour of the Canadian Arctic Gas Study proposal. This pressure to start a gas, and perhaps an oil pipe line as well, up the Mackenzie River Valley may be understandable if the most recent reserve estimates are valid. But in this case, the two enquiries would be something of a farce. Those who have reservations about the pipe line can only conclude that the authorities are determined to go ahead with the Canadian Arctic Gas Study proposal, and any views to the contrary – even questions about ecology and native rights – are to be discouraged.

If it seems we have not sufficient reserves to meet our own requirements, Canada must decide what to do about previously committed exports of natural gas. It is more difficult to cut out or phase out exports of natural gas than it is of oil. Gas exports are based on long-term contracts whereas oil exports have been on a month-to-month basis. And, moreover, pipe line systems have been built in the United States to transport gas from Canada. The federal government has the authority to curtail exports of natural gas if these were approved on the basis of incorrect estimates of our reserves. And the interests and requirements of Canadian consumers should definitely receive priority. Nevertheless, it is not an easy decision for the federal authorities. In the meantime, questions respecting the amount of our reserves and the general atmosphere of uncertainty are playing into the hands of the oil companies in their pleas for higher gas prices and their view of the urgent need to get on with the Mackenzie Valley gas pipe line.

What conclusions can be drawn from the foregoing recitation

of the reserves estimates by the National Energy Board and the oil industry in the last few years? The estimates of oil and gas reserves showed more than adequate supplies at a time when the Canadian Government was urging greater exports to the United States. The estimates plummeted in the short space of a year. Canadian officials are now talking about the need to curtail, not to increase, current export levels. The industry is urging considerable increases in the existing oil and gas prices (the former to the world price level), and for the abandonment of the two-price system. Although each estimate tended to bolster the objectives of the industry at the time, we should not over-emphasize this coincidence. Again, estimates of the potential reserves can be little more than educated guesses. Nevertheless, members of the public may be excused for being somewhat sceptical about the present and any future estimates.

The federal government and especially the Honourable Donald S. Macdonald and the Honourable John Turner are to be commended for the stands they took early in 1974 on the two-price system and on the taxation of the oil companies. However, the concessions made in connection with the Syncrude deal and the rumours that the government will soon approve an increase in oil prices, and perhaps gas prices, attests to the persuasiveness of industry spokesmen. The implication seems to be that if the major oil companies are not given further opportunities to make more money than they have been making in Canada, if the two-price system for oil is not abandoned, then the international giants, including their Canadian subsidiaries, may look for oil elsewhere.

When it comes to natural gas, the thrust of the industry's position seems to be that approval should be given to the Mackenzie Valley gas pipe line quickly. Otherwise, it is alleged, Canadians will go short of their requirements in a very few years' time.

The Canadian Government and the Canadian public should be sceptical about pressures of these kinds. Canadian industry in general, whose labour costs are getting out of line compared with labour costs and productivity across the border, badly needs the advantage in fuel costs provided by the present two-price system for oil in Canada. Moreover, if the price of oil in Canada is allowed to rise to world levels, Canadian consumers, faced as they are with serious inflation and a rising cost of living, will have to pay more for their fuel oil and their gasoline. The same conclusion applies in the case of natural gas.

Statements by oil company spokesmen should not be accepted at face value without further enquiry. These spokesmen are honourable men, and I am sure they believe sincerely in the points of view they put forward. But we should recognize that the major companies dominating the industry in this country are essentially branches of very large and very powerful international corporations. These circumstances are bound to influence to some extent, perhaps only indirectly, the opinions of their spokesmen in Canada.

It is axiomatic that in the last analysis the major oil companies in Canada primarily serve the interests of these international corporations which may not necessarily be the same as those of Canada. It is time we stopped being naive about the motives of the international oil companies and began to think about what is best for Canada.

Chapter 7 contains a proposal for dealing with the thirty-two largest foreign-controlled companies in Canada, including all the largest oil companies, without resorting to nationalization. I hope this proposal will be accepted. If not, then I believe Canadians would be wise to take over the foreign-controlled oil companies in Canada – or at least the largest of them, Imperial Oil – and turn their operations over to a Crown Corporation to be directed for and in the best interests of the Canadian people as a whole.

I do not suggest that the proposed Crown Corporation should be managed by civil servants. Its top officials could include a senior banker or someone from the private sector with a wide knowledge of finance, and an experienced Canadian operating executive from within the oil industry who was prepared to work in the best interests of our country. Given the right choice of top executives, I see no reason why such a set-up should not work quite satisfactorily. Apart from those at the very top, the existing organization of the companies should be kept intact. The relatively much smaller oil companies that are controlled in Canada should not be interfered with.

Chapter 6.

Foreign Economic Control and Influence

Since the Royal Commission on Canada's Economic Prospects submitted its reports in 1956 and 1957, there have been four more inquiries into the question of foreign economic control and influence. Three were sponsored by the Pearson and Trudeau governments and the fourth was conducted by a Select Committee of the Ontario Legislature.

The first of the federal government's reports, which became known as the Watkins Report, was submitted in January 1968. The Watkins task force, consisting solely of professional economists, was composed of Professor Melville Watkins of the University of Toronto, Chairman; Professors Abraham Rotstein, also of the University of Toronto; Bernard Bonin, Hautes Études Commercial, Montreal; A. E. Safarian, formerly of the University of Saskatchewan; the late Stephen Hymer of Yale; Claude Masson of Laval; Gideon Rosenbluth of the University of British Columbia; and W. J. Woodfine of St. Francis Xavier University. Possibly for the first time in the history of the profession, eight economists presented a unanimous report. This in itself was astounding to many observers. Moreover, the report's analysis and proposals ran counter to some of the established tenets of neo-classical economic theory, of which one of the greatest Canadian advocates has been Professor Harry Johnson of the University of Chicago who taught also at the London School of Economics. Johnson's persistent support of orthodox, if obsolescent beliefs, his tremendous energy, and his formidable debating style made him the spokesman for most university economists in Canada for a generation, despite his residence in Chicago. For the first time, eight respected academic economists, without ever mentioning Johnson by name, challenged his continentalist beliefs and thereby his influence in Canadian university circles.

The next report of a similar nature became known as the Wahn Report. Ian Wahn, QC, MP, was the Chairman of the House of Commons Committee on External Affairs and National Defence. The Committee made a study of the foreign investment (or Canadian independence) issue and made public its excellent report in August 1970.

Shortly before this, in the spring of 1970, the Trudeau government launched a third inquiry into the same subject under the chairmanship of the Honourable Herb Gray, Minister of National Revenue.

And finally in December 1971, the Government of Ontario appointed a Select Committee of the Ontario Legislature on Economic and Cultural Nationalism to examine the extent of foreign domination of Ontario's economy and culture and to make recommendations on future policy. The committee issued a number of reports over the ensuing three years and made many recommendations.

Each of these inquiries concluded that foreign-controlled Canadian companies do not operate necessarily in the best interests of Canada. According to the four reports, problems arise in such areas as:

☐ Resource extraction; depletion of Canadian non-renewable resources has occurred more rapidly than otherwise might have been the case;

☐ Export practices; foreign parent company policies sometimes determined by the laws of the country of the parent company, often restrict the opportunities of their Canadian subsidiaries to develop foreign markets for their products. This may be the result of restrictive licensing agreements and market share arrangements between the foreign parent firm and its Canadian subsidiary;

☐ Research and development; these functions are usually undertaken by the foreign parent company thus reducing or eliminating the opportunities for research and development in Canada;

☐ Purchasing policies; frequently these are developed to maximize the profits of the foreign parent company. This may mean that the Canadian subsidiary imports parts and components which could be produced in Canada, thus providing more job opportunities here. Moreover, inter-company pricing policies may tend to reduce the taxes otherwise payable in Canada;

☐ Disclosure of information; some Canadian subsidiary companies that are wholly owned by their foreign parent companies may not publish full details of their operations, which makes it difficult, if not impossible, to assess their impact and effects upon the Canadian economy;

☐ Hiring of Canadian managers and scientific personnel; in some cases, management talent is imported from the foreign parent company thus reducing the development of a pool of Canadian talent. In other cases, key management decisions are made by the foreign parent companies. This restricts the development and the responsibility of management personnel in the Canadian subsidiaries;

☐ Regional disparities; a problem of particular acuteness in Canada, but one which is less likely to be appreciated by foreign owners of Canadian companies;

☐ Various other problems including the payment of royalties and management fees, the determination of product lines, the processing of resources, the importation of advertising material, the rationalization of Canadian industry, the failure to develop a machinery and equipment industry in Canada, the composition of the teaching staffs of Canadian universities, and the ownership of Canadian land by foreigners.

These four investigative groups all recommended the creation of a special agency or administrative body (different names were suggested, but all the proposals amounted to the same thing), empowered to gather information and data pertaining to all facets of the foreign control of Canadian industries and to advise the government in developing policies to deal with the above-mentioned problems.

The reports suggested that this special agency, or the government itself, carefully review new ventures and the expansion of existing enterprises and facilities by foreign investors, particularly in the non-renewable resource industries of Canada. In the case of large ventures, it was suggested that the government be prepared to participate, if necessary, to ensure Canadian control.

Various measures were suggested to deal with the problem caused by restrictions on exports by Canadian subsidiaries due to laws and regulations of the countries of the foreign parent companies. These included, as a last resort, the creation of a Canadian exports trading corporation to conduct such export trade for foreign-owned Canadian companies. It was recommended that either government grants or tax incentives be used to encourage Canadian research and development. It was suggested that the special agency be empowered to compel the release of information, and to impose sanctions should foreign-owned companies refuse to comply with directives instructing them to bring their operations into conformity with Canadian interests.

Some long-term goals were suggested with respect to

the staffing of Canadian boards of directors and university teaching staffs.

The Watkins report endorsed the establishment of the Canada Development Corporation to help finance, either directly or through the organizing of consortia, large Canadian projects.

Further, it was suggested that tax incentives be given to encourage the sale of shares of foreign-owned companies to Canadians, and that Canadian guidelines be drawn up to counterbalance the guidelines formulated in the country of the foreign parent companies that now influence the operations of many subsidiaries in Canada. It was suggested also that the Canadian Government should promote mergers of smaller Canadian companies to achieve better rationalization of capacities.

These various recommendations and suggestions are impressive. But the overriding importance of the four reports lies not so much in their actual proposals, but that all four of them recognized the seriousness of the problem of foreign control in Canada. Despite this, governments have been more than hesitant to deal with the issue effectively.

The Pearson cabinet rejected the Watkins Report out of hand. The then Minister of Finance commented that it represented only the personal views of a few academics and had no bearing upon government policy. Other ministers thought the report should not be made public, although in the leaky Pearson cabinet little could be kept secret for very long. Eventually, it was decided to table the report but to make it clear the government took no responsibility whatever for its proposals. This was done. As I had been personally responsible for the creation of the task force and as I agreed with its conclusions, I felt compelled to resign in protest. This was my second resignation from the cabinet.

No action was taken by the government respecting the proposals of the Wahn Report, and nothing of consequence has been done about the Gray Report. Presumably, the reports of the Select Committee of the Ontario Legislature are still being digested by the Ontario Government.

While little legislative action has been taken so far, the net result of the publication of the Watkins Report in 1968, the Wahn Report in 1970, the Gray Report in 1972, and more recently the reports of the Select Committee of the Ontario Legislature has been to make at least some Canadians aware of the extent of foreign, mostly American, domination of our natural resources and business enterprises and its disadvantages. Moreover, there is evidence of a much more widespread popular concern about the issue.

As an example, Table 12 sets out the results of a poll on foreign investment released in March 1974 by the Public Opinion Institute of Canada (the Gallup Poll).

Table 12
PUBLIC OPINION INSTITUTE OF CANADA

"Would you favour or oppose legislation which would significantly restrict and control further foreign investment in Canada?"

	Favour	Partially Favour	Total	Don't Know
National	52%	17%	69%	13%
Atlantic	55	14	69	11
Quebec	46	13	59	20
Ontario	55	17	72	11
Prairies	51	20	71	10
British Columbia	53	24	77	7

A much more comprehensive survey that included responses from some twelve hundred individuals was conducted by the Elliott Research Corporation on behalf of the International Business Studies Research Unit of the University of Windsor in October and November 1974. Table 13 is taken from the report.

A substantial majority of those tested felt that foreign control, or rather U.S. control, of the economy is a bad thing for Canada. Those who felt this way were further tested "to investigate 'how much' of a lower standard of living Canadians would accept in order to abolish or reduce U.S. investment." Most of them said something between five and ten per cent although some went considerably higher. These views are significant. It should be emphasized, of course, that if in fact we were to take the steps required to regain control of the economy, the Canadian standard of living would be more likely to rise than to decline. I expect we would be surprised by the energies that would be released throughout the country if we managed to get rid of the present branch plant mentality in Canada.

The degree of regional uniformity of opinion as shown by these opinion polls should be kept in mind when statements are made that certain provincial politicians in Eastern and Western Canada are opposed to any action being taken on the Canadian economic independence issue.

In the light of such clear indications of public opinion, the federal government has made a number of gestures, including the creation of the Canadian Radio-Television Commission, which, under the chairmanship of Pierre Juneau has been struggling valiantly to see that there is a reasonable degree of Canadian content in our TV and radio programs. The government sponsored the Foreign Investment Review Act under which foreign takeovers of Canadian businesses are subject to review. So far, however, only a relatively small number of applications have been turned

Table 13
U.S. OWNERSHIP OF CANADIAN COMPANIES A GOOD OR BAD THING FOR OUR ECONOMY

BY AGE

	Total Canada	18-29	30-50	Over 50
Bad Thing	51.2%	57.7%	48.6%	46.6%
Good Thing	34.4	29.6	37.1	34.7
No opinion	14.4	12.7	14.3	18.7

BY PROVINCE OR REGION

	Total Canada	Atlantic	Quebec	Ontario	Prairies	British Columbia
Bad thing	51.2%	52.9%	48.5%	48.6%	58.0%	57.1%
Good thing	34.4	32.1	34.5	36.3	32.1	32.6
No opinion	14.4	15.0	17.0	15.1	9.9	10.3

down. The majority of the proposed takeovers have been approved. Another section of the Act which has not yet been proclaimed will require new foreign-controlled projects to be subject to the same scrutiny and approval.*

It should be fully understood, however, that this legislation, while useful in a limited way if applied more vigorously in future, does not come to grips with the problem of increasing foreign control of the economy. About eighty per cent of the increase in foreign control each year is represented by the expansion of existing foreign-controlled companies in Canada. These are not touched by the legislation.

The government plans to establish a Canadian oil company to be called Petrocan, which will compete with other companies in the development field. And at the time of writing, legislation is before Parliament to withdraw certain tax benefits from *Time* and *Reader's Digest* in an effort to give the Canadian magazine industry a more even chance competitively.

These initiatives are steps in the right direction, even though they do not come even close to achieving the objective of regaining a greater degree of economic independence. This will not be accomplished unless Parliament does something about the existing large foreign-controlled Canadian companies, which will be discussed in Chapter 7, and the foreign-controlled oil industry, which was discussed in Chapter 5.

According to the latest figures of Statistics Canada, the total book value of U.S. investment in Canadian industry amounted to $28 billion in August 1974. Of more importance, foreigners control many of our most dynamic industries including the following:

---

* This section of the act was proclaimed in the summer of 1975.

58% of all manufacturing
65% of mining
99% of petroleum refining
74% of oil and gas
96% of the automotive industry
98% of rubber
79% of chemicals
77% of electrical apparatus.

While the figures available from Statistics Canada are not up to date, those shown above should be sufficiently close for illustrative purposes.

Add to all this the oligopolistic structure of much of Canadian industry (described in Chapter 3) and it becomes apparent that the effective control of our economy by foreigners is even greater than the percentages shown above would indicate.

Our petroleum industry, for example, is in the stranglehold grip of eight large international oil companies. Our automobile industry is dominated by subsidiaries of the u.s. Big Three. The same pattern holds true in the computer and electrical apparatus industries and, to a lesser extent, in chemicals.

This means that in many of the more dynamic industries, one or more foreign-controlled companies set the pace. These companies establish the prices for industry products. But in doing so, they are influenced by neither the workings of a free market nor the kind of rate-setting bodies that have been established in such monopoly situations as railroads, telephone companies, and electric utilities. Obviously, they wield great economic power.

Foreign capital helped us to develop our economy more quickly than would otherwise have been possible. But now, we ourselves are generating much of the capital needed for further expansion. No longer do we need massive inflows of *equity* capital from abroad.

We may have difficulty in channeling sufficient Canadian savings into specific new developments like the James Bay project or the contemplated Mackenzie River Valley pipe line. If such is the case, and always assuming that such new developments are really in our own best interests at this time – and this can be disputed – we should insist that the foreign capital needed come in the form of fixed-term securities and not in the form of equity ownership. It is one thing to borrow the money needed to finance such projects; it can be paid back as profits are realized. It is quite another thing to allow foreigners to provide the necessary capital in a form that will permit them to own and therefore control the new developments indefinitely.

Much of the capital we are generating ourselves is represented by the retained earnings (net income less payment of dividends, etc.) of our larger corporations. And a great many of these corporations are controlled abroad. Thus, a large part of the total savings of Canadians (i.e. of the new capital that is generated in Canada) is accumulated by foreign-controlled subsidiary companies in Canada. This means Canadian savings are being used to increase foreign control of the economy.

To illustrate: the higher prices Canadians have been paying lately for gasoline and fuel oil have swelled the profits of Imperial Oil, Gulf, Shell, and other oil companies. A substantial part of these increased profits has been retained by the companies in question and reinvested in exploration and development. This in turn – to the extent such exploration is successful – increases the influence and control of these companies over the Canadian oil industry.

Despite the long debate over this issue, usually referred to as the foreign investment question or, more accurately, the Canadian independence issue, some people still ask

what are the specific disadvantages of the present degree of
foreign control of Canadian industry and Canadian
resources.

To begin with, we must acknowledge that business
leaders wield considerable influence in the formulation of
public policy. To the extent that these business leaders are
the chief executives of Canadian subsidiaries of U.S. or other
foreign corporations, they may, advertently or inadver-
tently, reflect the views and interests of such foreign corporations, which may not necessarily coincide with the best
interests of Canada. The fact is that our "branch plant mentality," occasioned by so much foreign control of Canada's
industry, has a stultifying effect on Canadian managers, scientists, and technicians.

As previously noted in commenting on the Watkins
and other reports, Canadian subsidiaries frequently are
required to rely on their foreign parents for research and
new product development, which is restricting insofar as
Canadian managers, scientists, and technicians are concerned. Such key decisions as expansion of markets, the
location of new plants, and the promotion of senior personnel are made at head office, usually in the United
States. This is not the best way to develop management
and scientific talent in Canada. And it reduces the number
of job opportunities for younger Canadian management
personnel.

Foreign-controlled companies in the manufacturing
field tend to import parts and components from their
parent corporations and associates instead of developing
alternative sources of supply in Canada and thereby creating more employment opportunities here. This is serious
and can become much more so. Ford of Canada, for
example, one of our two largest manufacturers, does not
even maintain a purchasing department in this country.
This means that a Canadian manufacturer who would like

to produce a certain part for the Canadian automobile industry has to convince someone at the Ford head office in Dearborn, Michigan, that he should be considered. Not an easy thing to do. Moreover, many Canadian subsidiaries of foreign parents are not permitted to develop export markets for their products, which again restricts employment opportunities in Canada.

The Northern Electric Company Limited (a subsidiary of Bell Canada) is a good example of what can happen to a Canadian company if it becomes dependent on its own resources. The operations of Northern Electric were patterned on Western Electric in the United States. While it was not owned in any formal sense by Western Electric, its operations were directed by that company in much the same way as are other Canadian subsidiaries. Then, in about 1965, it was decided the relationship should be changed and that Northern Electric should operate on its own. The senior management of the company faced up to this challenge with resolution and proceeded to reorganize and revitalize their company. They began to produce more parts and components in Canada, thus providing increased employment opportunities in this country and, at the same time, developed a considerable export business around the world. Northern Electric is now controlled and managed in Canada and is a company we can all be proud of. Sales have increased from $358 million, in 1965, to $971 million, in 1974. During the same period, the number of employees went up from 19,600 to 26,100. The achievements of the company's management group, once they were given a free hand, is an example of what could be accomplished in Canada on a much broader scale if the current branch plant philosophy was changed.

As was stated in Chapter 2, 61 of the 102 largest companies in Canada in the manufacturing, resource, and utility fields are controlled abroad. It is these large companies that expand and grow the fastest, and if changes are not made respecting their ownership, Canada is not likely to regain control of its economy. This is particularly true in the vitally important oil industry.

To suggest that we can gain control of our economy by encouraging new Canadian-controlled companies to enter the various fields in competition with the existing giants, and eventually to surpass them in importance, as is sometimes proposed, is extremely naive and hardly worthy of discussion. The fact of the matter is we cannot achieve the objective of regaining control of the Canadian economy unless ownership of the foreign-controlled Canadian companies (or the larger ones) is transferred to Canadians or to the Canadian Government. The various proposals for accomplishing this objective that have been put forward in the past have usually fallen into one of the following categories:

1. The nationalization of all or all of the larger foreign-controlled companies in Canada.
2. What is known as the key sector approach. The government, or a Crown Corporation on its behalf, would take control of one or more specific industries – such as the oil industry and the computer industry.
3. Some form of checking or monitoring of the operations of all, or all the larger, foreign-controlled companies in Canada. The government agency responsible for this should have full authority to require the companies in question to change their purchasing and other policies if this were thought desirable.

The main criticism of the above, and similar, proposals is the extent to which the government would have to intervene in the detailed working of the economy. Large sections of the public would find repugnant the idea of more bureaucratic direction and control and would also fear that nationalization on this scale might bring reprisals. It should be remembered that there are between seven and eight thousand (non-financial) companies in Canada controlled from abroad. If the operations of all these companies, or even all the larger ones, were to be directed or monitored by government authorities it would be a stupendous task.

Nevertheless, in the case of the oil industry, I would prefer the key sector approach to doing nothing at all about it. Under this approach, a Crown Corporation would take over and direct the operations of what are now the Canadian subsidiaries of the large international oil companies, or, failing that, the operations of by far the largest of these companies, Imperial Oil. The operations of the relatively much smaller Canadian-controlled companies should not be interfered with. I believe, however, that there is another approach to resolving the problem of foreign control of the Canadian economy that might be more acceptable to all concerned. I shall discuss this in the next chapter.

Before ending this chapter, it may be worth remarking that other countries also are concerned about foreigners acquiring too much influence in their economies through the acquisition of control of some of their important corporations. It is significant that members of the u.s. Congress have expressed anxiety that this may happen in their country. They seem particularly concerned that Arab nationals, who have tremendous funds at their disposal, will use them to buy control of u.s. corporations. There have been suggestions that Bills should be passed by Congress to prevent this. This being so, Americans in public life should readily understand Canadian concern about what has already happened here and our desire to rectify the situation.

At a recent Canadian-u.s. seminar in St. Paul, Minnesota, William McKinley Johnson, the deputy chief of Mission at the U.S. embassy in Ottawa was reported as saying that at a conservative estimate, more than twenty-seven per cent of the total Canadian capital plant is owned by U.S. interests. He conceded that this statistic alone is justification for considerable concern on the part of Canadians about control of their economic destiny. We can appreciate Mr. Johnson's perception about our anxieties. The time has surely come for us to do something about the matter. No one else is going to do it for us.

Chapter 7.

How to Regain our Economic Independence

In the last chapter I outlined some of the disadvantages we suffer from in Canada, because so many of our business enterprises and so much of our natural resources are controlled by foreigners. Now I shall present a relatively simple plan, which I believe would come to grips effectively with the foreign control issue – with a minimum of fuss. Towards the end of the chapter, I shall put forward a number of tax and other proposals designed to give Canadian-controlled companies a better break. Taken together, these proposals should give the whole Canadian business community, the whole Canadian economy, a new lease on life.

The approach chosen should be fair to those who invested their money in this country in good faith, and, to the extent possible, it should avoid charges of retroactive legislation. It should also be as simple as possible.

Specifically, I suggest that Members of Parliament express by resolution the view that the foreign owners of the larger Canadian subsidiary companies should, gradually over a period of years, sell out to Canadians. I would hope this could be done by a free vote so that members of all

This chapter is based in part on an article by Walter L. Gordon in the October 5, 1974, issue of *The Financial Post*.

political parties could find it politically convenient to support the resolution, which I suggest should stipulate the stages in which the objective should be accomplished.

The resolution should define what is meant by the "larger" Canadian subsidiary companies. I would suggest this should include all companies with assets in excess of $250 million. At the end of 1973, there were only 32 of them, which would make the problem manageable. But a transfer of control of these 32 large companies would mean that, at long last, we would be dealing with the issue in a forthright and effective way. The seven or eight thousand other foreign-controlled Canadian companies would be left completely alone unless and until their total assets reached the $250 million mark.

The 32 foreign-controlled companies that would be included in my list are:

Imperial Oil Ltd.
Gulf Oil Canada Ltd.
Shell Canada Ltd.
Texaco Canada Ltd.
Texaco Exploration Canada Ltd.
BP Canada Ltd.
Petrofina Canada Ltd.
Hudson's Bay Oil & Gas
Pacific Petroleums
Amoco Canada Petroleum
Husky Oil
Interprovincial Pipe Lines
Westcoast Transmission
Canadian International Paper
Crown Zellerbach Canada Ltd.
B.C. Forest Products Ltd.
Rio Algom Mines
Falconbridge Nickel
Hudson Bay Mining & Smelting

General Motors of Canada Ltd.
Ford of Canada Ltd.
Chrysler Canada Ltd.
Canadian Industries Ltd.
Du Pont of Canada Ltd.
Canadian General Electric Co.
IBM Canada Ltd.
Canada Cement Lafarge
Anglo Canadian Telephone
Rothmans of Pall Mall Canada Ltd.
Imasco
Genstar
I.T. & T., Canadian interests.

I suggest the various stages in which control of these 32 companies should be transferred to Canadians – which should be spelled out in the House of Commons Resolution – should be as follows:

Stage one: To take place within a year or eighteen months and apply to companies in the resource sector with total assets in excess of $2 billion. Imperial Oil would be the only one to qualify. The quoted market value of the seventy per cent of its shares held by Exxon was about $2.25 billion at the end of March of 1975.

Stage two: To take place within three years and apply to companies in the resource sector with total assets exceeding $1 billion. Only two companies would be involved: Gulf Oil Canada and Shell Canada. The quoted market value of the approximately seventy per cent of the shares of these companies owned by their foreign parent corporations would amount to about $1.5 billion.

Stage three: To take place within five years and apply also to companies in the resource field with assets exceeding $500 million. These would include Texaco

Canada, Canadian International Paper, Amoco Canada Petroleum, Pacific Petroleums, Westcoast Transmission and Falconbridge Nickel. The shares of two of these are not quoted on the stock exchanges. However, at a rough guess, the six companies together might be worth about $2 billion.

Stage four: To take place within seven years and apply to manufacturing and commercial companies with total assets exceeding $1 billion. These would include Ford of Canada Ltd., General Motors of Canada Ltd. and Anglo Canadian Telephone. Total quoted market value of Ford and Anglo Canadian on March 31, 1975, was approximately $600 million. GM Canada's shares are not listed, but their net book value according to the company's balance sheet on December 31, 1973, was $443 million. Taken altogether, these three companies might be worth about $1.25 billion.

Stage five: To take place within ten years, and apply to all other foreign-controlled companies with total assets exceeding $250 million. These would include: Chrysler Canada Ltd., Canadian General Electric Co., IBM Canada Ltd., Canadian Industries Ltd., Rothmans of Pall Mall Canada Ltd., Petrofina Canada Ltd., Rio Algom Mines, BP Canada Ltd., Du Pont of Canada Ltd., Crown Zellerbach Canada Ltd., Canada Cement Lafarge, B.C. Forest Products, Husky Oil, Interprovincial Pipe Lines, Hudson Bay Mining & Smelting, Texaco Exploration Canada Ltd., Hudson's Bay Oil & Gas, Imasco, Genstar and the Canadian assets of I.T. & T. As a guess, the total value of this group might amount to about $4.5 billion.

Altogether, the above estimates come to $11.5 billion or, to be safe, say, about $15 billion to be paid by Canadian investors (not the Canadian Government) over a period of ten years. This amount should be well within Canada's financial capabilities.

However, it would be up to the owners to decide how the changes in control should be accomplished. In many cases, this would simply be a matter of selling the shares of their Canadian subsidiaries for cash through underwriters. In some cases, the Canada Development Corporation or some new federal or provincial agencies, established for the purpose, might buy control. In still others, it might be necessary to sell control, not for cash, but for some form of debentures redeemable over a term of years.

In all cases, it would be important to stipulate changes in the share structure of the companies to provide that, after the change of control, not more than twenty-five per cent of the shares in total could be held by foreigners, and not more than ten per cent by any single foreigner or associated group. This is the formula provided in the Bank Act respecting foreign holdings of shares of the Canadian chartered banks. It should be incorporated in the proposed Parliamentary Resolution.

The advantages of this proposal would be that:

1. No legislation would be required and there would be no need for sanctions. Obviously, if the proposed Resolution by Members of Parliament was ignored, the government would have to take action at some later date. But this would seem to be unlikely.
2. Only 32 companies would be affected.
3. The companies would not be nationalized.
4. It would be left to the foreign owners to decide how to go about selling the shares of their subsidiaries to Canadians.
5. They would have plenty of time to work things out.
6. For all practical purposes, the transfer of ownership of these 32 large companies would resolve the foreign control issue. The remaining seven or eight thousand

smaller foreign-controlled companies in Canada would not be involved in any way.

Despite the above advantages, there would be criticisms of this or any other plan. In the past, when proposals have been made to repatriate or, as some people now say with pejorative overtones, "buy back" control of Canadian companies controlled by foreigners, critics have said that this would mean using Canadian capital that could otherwise have been used for other enterprises. There is some validity in this, although whether such capital would be "better" used is open to question.

Other critics may claim that the sudden withdrawal of substantial amounts of capital invested here could have a depressing effect on the exchange rate for the Canadian dollar. This might be true. On the other hand, there are those who fear strong upward pressures on the Canadian dollar in the next few years, arising from forign capital inflows to finance some major projected developments in the resource field. One of these influences might be expected to offset the others. Apart from this, our foreign exchange reserves are near their record high and could be used to cushion the effects of sudden capital outflows.

It should not be overlooked, moreover, that Canadian portfolio investments abroad are quite considerable. Part of these investments by pension funds, mutual funds, and individuals was invested in the United States and other countries because of a shortage of high quality common stocks available for investment in Canada. If the supply of common stocks in Canada was increased significantly as a result of the foregoing proposal, it is probable that a proportion of Canadian portfolio investments abroad would be sold and the proceeds brought home for investment here. If it so wished, the government could provide incentives to stimulate this trend.

Quite apart from these considerations, if it became necessary, the government or its agencies presumably could borrow money in the United States or other countries from time to time to offset some of the capital funds to be withdrawn from Canada. In this way some part of the foreign *equity* capital now invested in Canadian industry would be replaced by foreign capital invested in fixed term government securities.

There will be other criticisms of this proposal as there always are about any new ideas. There will be those who say we cannot afford to use our capital resources in this way; that any attempt to repatriate control of our larger companies is regressive, not forward looking. There are others who see nothing to be gained by exchanging foreign owners of these companies for Canadian. We know the socialists' refrain: What is the difference between a Canadian capitalist and an American capitalist? And there are those who are afraid of doing anything that might provoke the American authorities.

People in most other industrialized countries would laugh at such criticisms. They might say we were foolish to have allowed such massive foreign control of our economy to occur in the first place. But they probably would add that for such a rich and prosperous country as Canada to permit this foreign control to continue would be the height of folly and quite unnecessary.

It would be difficult to claim that the cost of regaining effective control of the Canadian economy is beyond our financial capacity. Quite obviously, this is not the case. Only 32 companies would be affected. It would cost about $15 billion over a period of ten years, but part of this could be financed by the issue of bonds and debentures redeemable over a longer period. One thing is clear: the longer we put off doing something, the more expensive and the more difficult the task will be.

There are those who are concerned, and rightly so, by the control exercised by the top officers of the international trade unions over the operations of their Canadian locals. This concern is shared by many Canadian trade unionists who would like to have more to say about their own affairs. But I have always thought that the close and intimate relationships of the larger Canadian subsidiaries and their foreign parents should be severed first. Once this has been done, it should be easier and more appropriate to start worrying about the international unions. My guess is that this will be done and should be done, when the time comes, by Canadian trade unionists themselves.

There are a few more suggestions about the Canadian independence issue that should be touched on briefly. To begin with, I should like to say a few words about our tax system as it applies to corporations. Foreigners doing business in Canada through Canadian subsidiaries have many advantages over their Canadian competitors, apart altogether from their larger size and ready access to finances. Therefore it would seem reasonable for such advantages to be offset to some degree by giving Canadian-controlled companies some preferred treatment in our tax laws. I suggest that the tax rate for Canadian-controlled companies should be ten percentage points lower than the rate for other companies. In other words, if the normal rate of tax for companies in Canada were fifty per cent, the rate for Canadian-controlled companies would be forty per cent.

Canadian-controlled companies should be permitted to amortize their capital expenditures against taxable income at any rate they may determine. This would make it easier for such Canadian-controlled companies to keep their plant and equipment up-to-date and, except possibly in the first year or so, would not cost the federal treasury very much.

This suggestion would give Canadian-controlled companies one advantage over their foreign-controlled competitors who have them at a disadvantage in so many other ways.

For taxation purposes, I suggest that a "Canadian controlled company" be defined as one with not more than twenty-five per cent of its shares held by foreigners and not more than ten per cent of its shares held by a single foreigner or associated group. This, of course, would include all the chartered banks (with the exception of Mercantile unless the Bank Act is changed to make it comply with this rule). It would not apply to such companies as Canadian Pacific or International Nickel, however, because, while more than fifty per cent of their shares are now held in Canada, over twenty-five per cent of them are held by residents of other countries. If it were thought to be desirable, Section 168 of the Canada Business Corporations Act could be amended to permit any Canadian company to place constraints on the transfer of its shares to non-residents if more than fifty per cent of its shares are held by Canadians at the time of approval of such constraints. In that event, such companies should qualify as "Canadian-controlled companies" for tax purposes. Not all companies who might qualify would wish this as it would reduce the marketability of their shares. On the other hand, the tax incentive resulting from being classed as a Canadian-controlled company would be substantial under the proposal outlined above.

In the fiscal year 1972-73, the federal government spent about $250 million in grants of various kinds to industry. Much of this went to companies controlled by foreigners. If we are serious about regaining control of our economy, all such grants in future should go to Canadian-controlled companies. If the main proposal put forward in this chapter was implemented, for all practical purposes the Canadian economic independence issue would be settled within a decade.

There are, of course, other important matters to be determined relating to the whole broad question of foreign control and influence in Canada. In the cultural field, there is the question of book publishing, of American produced text books used in some elementary schools, which proclaim for example that George Washington was the Father of our country; of the preferred position of *Time* and *Reader's Digest* (now at long last being changed); and the controversy over too many foreign nationals on the teaching staffs of Canadian universities. There is also the question of the ownership of land by foreigners. These matters have not been touched on, because in dealing with domestic policies, this book has been restricted to economic issues.

Chapter 8.

Federal-Provincial Controversies

One of Canada's basic difficulties at present stems from conflicts between federal and provincial governments over their respective areas of responsibility and authority. Similar differences in some other confederations, notably the United States, have been settled over the years in favour of the federal authorities. This has not been the case in Canada.

A number of appeals were made to the British Privy Council to interpret the Canadian constitution – the British North America Act – on various important issues. But these appeals were determined in the main in favour of the provinces. Since appeals to the Privy Council were abolished, several attempts at federal-provincial conferences to amend the constitution have proved to be abortive. Canadian governments, federal and provincial, have not been able even to agree upon a formula for amending the constitution without application to the British Parliament.

This legal stalemate has not prevented some necessary changes taking place in practice. During World War II, for example, it was essential for the federal government to assume authority in various fields including that of taxation. The positive action that was taken was approved by the general public despite some squawking by a few of the provincial governments. Very properly, these wartime powers were surrendered once the hostilities were over. In the succeeding three decades, there have been an increasing number of federal-provincial conferences at which, of course, the federal representatives have been outnumbered ten to one. Partly because of this, the provinces have gradually acquired more and more power at the expense of the federal authorities.

Inevitably and inexorably, the federal government has been weakened to the point where it cannot easily discharge its responsibilities in the economic field.

While the increasing degree of consultation with the provinces has been beneficial in some ways and should be continued, it seems time for the pendulum to start swinging back in favour of a stronger federal government. This is particularly important when the world is in a period of crisis; when our relations with the United States may become more and more difficult as that country increasingly needs and covets our resources of all kinds including oil, gas, uranium and fresh water; as it becomes increasingly apparent that it is imperative for Canada to regain control of the foreign corporations that presently wield far too much power and influence in our country; and as it becomes obvious that new approaches are needed to contain inflation and to provide new opportunities for employment. Only the federal government can deal effectively with these problems. They are beyond the capabilities of ten provinces acting independently of each other.

Some time after the Trudeau government first came to power, a Joint Committee of the Senate and the House of Commons was established to study the constitution and recommend changes. This Committee, under the joint chairmanship of Gildas Molgat and Mark MacGuigan, presented its report in the spring of 1972, a few months before the Liberal government's near defeat in the October election of that year. The Committee recommended a new and distinctively Canadian constitution. It recommended that social and cultural affairs should be the responsibility of the provinces and that there should be a greater centralization at the federal level of those powers that bear on economic matters.

In listing the principal criticisms it had heard in the course of its public meetings, the Committee emphasized that the federal Parliament does not have sufficient power to manage and plan the economy nor to cope with large multinational corporations, international unions, and the overwhelming influence and power of the United States. The Committee stated that to control foreign ownership, the federal authority should have paramount powers, including those of nationalizing industries and expropriating land and resources threatened by takeover.

Obviously, it was impossible for the Trudeau minority government to do anything about the MacGuigan-Molgat report in the days following the 1972 election, and there is not now time to wait for a formal resolution of Canada's constitutional difficulties before dealing with our present pressing problems. Thus the best course would be for the federal government, which once again has the support of a working majority of the members, to assert itself, something it would be much more difficult, if not impossible, for a minority government to do. If the present government in Ottawa does not do this there may never be another chance.

To be specific, I believe the federal authorities should state firmly their intention to take a number of initiatives in order to fulfil their responsibilities in the economic field. These initiatives should include their plans respecting foreign control of the Canadian oil industry and of Canadian industry in general, their proposals for providing more jobs, for containing inflation and the various other suggestions and proposals that have been outlined in this book.

At the same time, the federal government should reaf-

firm its willingness to transfer to the provinces full responsibility for both the administration and the financing of all
joint programs in the social security field, with the exception of unemployment insurance and the Canada Pension
Plan. The principle for such transfers was established
under the Opting Out legislation of 1965. This legislation
gave to any province that so wished the right to take full
responsibility for certain specified joint programs. Only
Quebec has done so. This opportunity should now be
extended to include medicare and the Canada Assistance
Act, which were subsequently approved by Parliament. To
make this attractive, the federal government might have to
increase slightly the number of tax points allocated to the
provinces now provided for under the Opting Out formula.
(To provide for medicare and the provisions of the Canada
Assistance Act, it would be necessary to do so anyway.)

The federal government should agree also to allow the
provinces to modify to some extent the present social
security benefits. For example, if some provinces would
like to charge those people who can afford it a modest fee
for every day spent in hospital as a deterrent against
staying on unnecessarily, why should they not be allowed
to do so? Moreover, the needs of people living in a New-
foundland outport, for example, differ from those of people living in Vancouver or other metropolitan centres
where living conditions are not the same. Why should this
not be recognized?

A good case can be made that the provincial governments are in a better position to determine the details of
what their people need and want in the field of social
security than the federal government, which is not as close
to them. Canada would not have the social security system
it now has – one that while not perfect by any means is
something we can take pride in – if it had not been for
initiatives taken by the federal authorities. But now the

system is established, it would make sense to turn over full responsibility to the provinces not only for the administration of the programs, but also for imposing the taxes required to pay for them.

Provinces that do not wish to assume responsibility for financing these social security programs should not be forced to do so, even if the federal government is willing to make room for them in the division of the tax revenue fields. The Atlantic provinces, for example, might be reluctant to do so. But every inducement should be given to Ontario and the other richer provinces to follow Quebec's lead.

While the federal government should retain full responsibility for unemployment insurance (and the Canada Pension Plan), it should take steps to clear up certain anomalies that bring discredit on this and other programs in the social security field. In *The Globe and Mail* on April 4, 1975, Scott Young referred to an interview with Statistics Canada and stated: "In the 1973 figures, $686,000 in unemployment insurance went to Canadians with declared incomes of $25,000 a year and above; $20,000 of that going to persons with incomes in excess of $50,000 a year." He went on to say that the above "is unlikely to provide solace for anyone . . . who pays taxes to provide money used for such incomprehensible ends."

It does not make sense that people like generals or bank managers, for example, are entitled to draw unemployment insurance for one year after retirement in addition to their pensions. Nor does it make sense that a seasonal worker who has made, say, $20,000 or $25,000 in the preceding six months should be entitled to draw unemployment insurance benefits in the next six months while holidaying in Florida or elsewhere. These are the kind of things that should be corrected.

I am quite convinced that a great majority of Canadians

are vitally anxious that their country should continue as a
separate sovereign state, and I believe the proposals outlined
in this book, especially those aimed at regaining control of
the economy, are essential if this is to be achieved. The various proposals for changes in economic policies – the proposed assertion of authority by the federal government in
order to implement them; and a willingness to transfer responsibility to the provinces in the social security field –
could be presented as a very impressive program. While parts
of it might be opposed by some provincial governments, for
example the recently elected government in Alberta, it should
add up to a comprehensive set of policies for or other of the
two principal political parties at the next election.

It is not my purpose, of course, to suggest a program
or a strategy for any political party despite the fact that I
am a member of the Liberal Party and had a hand in
formulating the policies that brought the Liberals back to
power after their devastating defeats in the 1957 and 1958
elections. I am no longer concerned with partisan politics.
What is of paramount importance, however, is that we adopt
the kind of policies that will be necessary if Canada is to regain and then retain its independence as a separate sovereign
nation. This cannot be accomplished by ten provincial governments acting independently and sometimes at cross purposes. If the objective of regaining and then retaining our independence is to be achieved, the power and authority of the
federal government must first be re-established. I believe this
to be a major challenge of the present government. If it fails
to meet it, sooner or later our country may very well disinte-
grate. If that should happen, it would be small comfort to
be able to blame the Trudeau administration for failing to
prevent it.

Chapter 9.

Canadian
Foreign Policy

Because of Canada's important contributions in two world wars and because of the initiatives taken in the decade or so following World War II, by Prime Minister Louis St. Laurent, and the special personal and other qualities of Lester B. Pearson, his Secretary of State for External Affairs, this country achieved a recognition throughout the world somewhat out of proportion to our position in terms of population and relative power. This was a period Canadians look back on with feelings of nostalgia. Now the physical possession of raw materials and food supplies is of even greater importance than it was in the past and Canada is fortunate in these respects. In this current period of world uncertainties, of shortages of raw material, of fear, and of dangerous power politics, not to mention the fact that more nations possess, or soon will possess, the atom bomb, Canada's main preoccupation in foreign affairs must be to regain a greater degree of independence as a separate sovereign state. Other considerations apart, this would be appropriate to her position as a leading producer of key resources.

This means that while we should continue to be interested and involved with everything that goes on anywhere in this troubled and anarchic world, our paramount consideration must be our relationships with the United States. This must always be, as far into the future as anyone can see, the overriding preoccupation of our foreign policy. It will not be an easy preoccupation if Canadians wish to maintain their independence, in fact as well as in name.

This – the main emphasis in our foreign policy – should not become a partisan political issue and it never should be permitted to take on anti-American overtones. The Americans are our friends and allies. We are lucky indeed to have them for our neighbours. But this does not mean we should allow them to dominate us in the economic or any other fields; we must stand up for our own interests when occasions call for it.

The Canadian Government has done a number of things in the area of foreign policy in the last six years, most of which should be commended. I should like to begin this chapter by discussing these recent initiatives. To begin with, there was the much-heralded internal foreign policy review that took place from 1968 to 1970. It concluded with the publication of *Foreign Policy for Canadians*, six slim volumes that were criticized immediately, because they did not include a comprehensive statement of what Canada's policies should be towards the United States. Canadians know instinctively that this must be the main focus of our foreign policy, and yet it was not emphasized in the government statements.

Moreover, morale was low in the Department of External Affairs at a time when the departments concerned with economic matters became the focus of policy-making. Some experienced senior officers either were not consulted about the review of foreign policy or their suggestions were not accepted. Some of them were passed over when it came to postings they had been promised; others were retired early or moved to other positions within the civil service. External Affairs was no longer considered by the Ottawa hierarchy as the senior and somewhat exalted department it had been previously.

The lukewarm reception of *Foreign Policy for Canadians* was followed a bit belatedly by a statement on Canadian-American relations in which emphasis was placed on what was called the "Third option" – the formation of "a comprehensive, long-term strategy to develop and strengthen the Canadian economy and other aspects of our national life and in the process to reduce the present Canadian vulnerability" to American influence. The emphasis in this statement on the need for cultivating a distinct Canadian presence in North America without running counter to u.s. global policy seemed sensible enough. But to the extent it meant diversifying Canada's trade away from the United States, it seemed rather more wishful in its thinking than realistic, especially as it made no specific suggestions as to how this should be accomplished.

At the same time as the foreign policy review was in progress, the government was engaged in a reassessment of Canada's defence policy and, in particular, of the Canadian NATO contribution. The April 1969 decision to reduce the Canadian force in Europe was commendable. Following strong protests from our European allies, the government decided upon a cut of about fifty per cent. This reduction of one-half of our NATO forces demonstrated both to the Canadian public and to our foreign allies that henceforth Canada would judge its military commitments abroad in terms of a continuing analysis of what seemed best for Canada. The new European affluence and Canada's own changing security requirements in North America provided two strong arguments for reducing, if not terminating, Canada's physical presence in Europe.

In the light of hindsight, it is fortunate that we remained an active and concerned member of the NATO group. Subsequent events, such as the continuing armaments build-up by the Soviet Union (especially their rapid deployment of naval strength), and aggressive Soviet behaviour during the Arab-Israeli conflict of October 1973, indicate that peace in Europe is not wholly certain and that the Western deterrent in that zone must remain credible. Because of this a continuing symbolic contribution by Canada to NATO's European forces may be required at least until such time as the Mutual Force Reductions negotiations are successful in winning a meaningful cut in Soviet and Warsaw Pact forces stationed in Eastern Europe.

Equally significant is Europe's recent economic weakness following the massive rise in oil prices and the growing realization in Europe that it should have rearmed conventionally at a greater rate when it possessed the economic freedom to do so. The European states are now under the double pressure of maintaining their domestic economies in the face of balance of payments difficulties caused by oil purchases at very high prices while having to allocate significant portions of their budgets to the next generation of modern weaponry (for example the recent commitment to purchase some 350 American F-16 fighter aircraft by Norway, Denmark, Belgium and the Netherlands at a cost of about $2 billion). To the extent that we in Canada continue to recognize that there is a need to join in the defence of Western Europe, we should continue to maintain a noticeable force to help maintain European security. Even token forces can contribute to the psychological impact of the Western European deterrent. And psychological impact is, of course, at the root of the concept of deterrence.

Canada's recognition of the People's Republic of China on October 13, 1970, marked a significant contribution to the international scene. At the time the decision was taken in 1968 to move towards recognition of the People's Republic, the United States was still strongly opposed to such an act. It took courage, diplomatic skill (and also perhaps a change in American attitudes) to bring about the desired establishment of relations with Peking. It seems reasonable to attribute to Canada's move some credit for the eventual Sino-American rapprochement beginning with Henry Kissinger's visit to Peking in the summer of 1971. Once China's emissaries were resident in Ottawa, it was quite common and convenient for American officials to visit the Chinese embassy to sound out the prospects for the establishment of mutual diplomatic ties. In addition to facilitating the new Sino-American understanding, the Canadian move precipitated several other acts of recognition by Western countries, helped draw the Chinese out of their isolation, and thereby eventually contributed to a more stable international order. The recognition of the People's Republic was certainly long overdue (St. Laurent and Pearson had, after all, wanted to establish contact with Peking, but the Korean War and political circumstance first at home, then in China had prevented it), but it is nevertheless very much to the Trudeau government's credit that it carried out this action.

In 1970, the government formulated another strong response, this time to the threat of the ecology of Canada's Arctic and the challenge to her sovereignty posed by the voyages of the supertanker *Manhattan* in 1969 and 1970. With the passage of the Arctic Waters Pollution Prevention Act and the extension of Canada's territorial sea to twelve nautical miles through amendment of other legislation, the government provided the basis for control over all Arctic shipping through the Canadian archipelago. Since the United States government objected and continues to object strenuously to both the one-hundred mile pollution control zone and the effective closing of the Northwest Passage (except by way of innocent passage and under Canadian anti-pollution regulations), it is important that this claim be fortified by international recognition. Mr. Trudeau attempted unsuccessfully to win Soviet support for the Arctic pollution-control concept during his 1971 visit to the Soviet Union. But where Canada was unsuccessful in a bilateral context with Russia it may prove successful in the multilateral context of the Law of the Sea Conference. In any case, the unilateral declaration of the Arctic Waters Act's provisions and the measures contained in the various amendments to the Territorial Sea and Fishing Zones Act have provided important reinforcement to the case for unchallenged Canadian sovereignty north of sixty degrees of latitude.

Given the importance of this claim, the government should back it up with a substantial physical Canadian presence in the Arctic zone. The use of Canadian military personnel in a greatly expanded northern role of sovereignty protection is therefore of prime importance, as is the much-mooted acquisition of a fleet of northern ice breakers.

Canada's 1970 position on control of the territorial sea that emerged in connection with Arctic waters pollution was subsequently extended and embellished. This took place at the third United Nations Conference on the Law of the Sea in sessions at Caracas, Venezuela, and then Geneva, Switzerland. At the time of writing, the results of that conference remain to be determined.

The proposals for a two hundred-mile "exclusive economic zone" and a twelve-mile territorial sea originated with the developing countries of Latin America, but Canada seems to have appropriated them. These seem to have been popular moves at the conference and appear likely to gain acceptance. If they do, it should validate beyond question the Canadian claims for controlling the seas in the Far North.

Canada's general attitude to the war in Vietnam during the Pearson administration has been severely criticized. It was said that our representatives on the International Control Commission were less objective, less non-partisan than they should have been. However, our representatives did provide a communication link between Washington and Hanoi, which was useful and important. Prime Minister Pearson frequently spoke out against the war though it must be admitted his statements were often so qualified it was difficult for members of the general public to understand their import. He was more than usually explicit in a speech at Temple University in April 1965 when he urged the United States to stop the bombing of North Vietnam at least temporarily in the hope that this might encourage peace negotiations. For his effort, he received a personal dressing down from President Lyndon B. Johnson that some of those present have said barely stopped at fisticuffs.

On balance, however, the government gave the impression that Canada was supporting the United States in what was an unpopular and quite unnecessary war. Canada was benefitting from the Defence Production Sharing Agreement, although not to any great extent, and while we had refused to send even a token force to South Vietnam, our attitude appeared as if we favoured the Americans in their participation in what was basically a civil war in Indo-China.

The Canadian public did not support the government in this attitude. This was made crystal clear in May 1967. I had made a carefully worded speech criticizing the war in Vietnam and urging the United States to stop the bombing of the North. My words were free of the usual qualifications, however, and the media made a big thing of it. Some of my colleagues in the Cabinet felt I should be dismissed for this expression of a personal opinion, and a special meeting was called to consider the matter. But my speech provoked an unprecedented response in terms of mail, almost all of which was favourable. It was clear the public supported the stand that I had taken. After that, the position of the Canadian government stiffened noticeably.

All this was part of the background in 1972 when it became clear before the signing of the Paris armistice agreement that Canada would be asked to participate in the new control commission, the International Commission of Control and Supervision for Vietnam (ICCS). Canada could not properly shirk this international responsibility and did not do so. Michel Gauvin, then our Ambassador to Greece, was designated to lead our delegation and he proved an admirable choice. He is not a man who can be pushed around. When this was attempted, he let the whole world know about it in no uncertain terms. To make a long story short, Canada accepted a role on the ICCS provisionally; once the United States had successfully obtained the release of its prisoners of war, Canada stated clearly and unequivocally that the ICCS was impotent to make an effective contribution to the peace, and resigned.

The Canadian position was determined throughout by a clear-headed assessment of the Canadian interest. The decision to accept a role was made in light of Canadian desires to help effect an American withdrawal from Vietnam. It was appreciated from the beginning that "peace with honour" might prove to be merely diplomatic rhetoric to permit an American withdrawal without complete loss of face. It was appreciated also that this might be the sole means of extricating a U.S. administration that, while arrogant and boastful in its utterances, was rapidly losing credibility. Given those circumstances it was clearly in Canadian interests to help the United States out of a war that many, if not most, Canadians had long since condemned as a wholly immoral exercise of American force.

A strong sense of what is in Canada's best interests need not be and should not be anti-American in its manifestations. Rather, it should be a level-headed appreciation of where long-term Canadian interests lie and how best these interests might be served. Promoting the U.S. departure from Indo-China and the end of the tragic and socially destructive participation in that war could only serve Canada's long-term interests. At the same time, ending the Canadian participation on what was essentially an ineffectual and costly Commission was equally in our interests, no matter how much the Americans were likely to protest. By July 1973, the primary task had been completed; the withdrawal of American prisoners was finished. In a complex and difficult situation, such decisions were illustrative of a prudent and sensible approach by the Canadian Government towards defining the Canadian national interest.

The final event I would draw attention to is the very recent decision to restructure the operations of the North American Air Defence Command (NORAD). In the new system, peacetime control of Canadian airspace will be monitored solely by Canadian personnel. Until now, responsibility for the surveillance and control of airspace in Western Canada was assigned to American-based aircraft. The construction of a new regional NORAD base at Edmonton, to begin in 1976, is another small step towards emphasizing Canadian sovereignty. But there remains the basic question of whether the NORAD arrangement is needed any longer. It has been pointed out repeatedly since the mid-1960's that the whole concept of anti-bomber defence is absurd given the existence of a massive arsenal of ballistic missiles in the Soviet Union.

The government recently decided to renew the NORAD agreement in its restructured form, subject to cancellation on one year's notice. Perhaps it seemed inadvisable to create a controversy with the Americans over an issue that may be of less importance than some of the economic questions on which our respective points of view may differ. If this is so, the position of the government is understandable. However, the longer we remain in NORAD, the more likely it seems the Department of National Defence will opt for purchases of new jet aircraft rather than the naval vessels (and

the icebreakers) some critics believe to be more important –
always assuming the defence budget will not extend to both.
My own opinion is that the sooner Canada pulls out of what
is now an obsolete arrangement the better it will be.

So much for the background and a recital of some of the
new initiatives taken in the last six years. From now on, as
already intimated, the main preoccupation of our foreign
policy (which must be in phase with our economic policies)
will be with our relations with the United States. We can
expect differences to arise and pressures to be applied over
oil and natural gas, over uranium and other energy sources
and, quite possibly, over access to Canadian supplies of fresh
water. The latter question, more than others, seems to upset
Canadians emotionally. There may be serious differences
over the free passage of American oil tankers through what
we assert are Canadian territorial waters in the North and
over definitions as to what are and what are not our rights in
the Continental Shelf, which, at some points, extends for several hundred miles off shore. There will be other sensitive issues including the measures Canada will have to take to bring
our trade and other transactions with the United States into
better balance. This could entail substantial amendments to,
or the abrogation of, the auto pact.

And, finally, there is the kind of action advocated in
this book for regaining a greater measure of control over
the economy. The reasons for this should be carefully
explained to everyone concerned from the President of the
United States down. And I would hope that the procedure
suggested in Chapter 7 – a strong expression of opinion
by members of all parties in a free vote in the House of
Commons and the fact it was contemplated that the
changes would take place gradually over a ten-year period
– would be accepted as being fair and reasonable. Such an
approach would be very different from the sudden take-

over of foreign companies that has occurred in many other countries. All these issues will call for careful handling and perhaps new methods and new techniques for explaining Canadian positions, not only to the appropriate officials in Washington but also to the media and members of the Congress.

Through it all, Canada must continue to play its part in the world, especially in the field of aid, primarily food, to the underdeveloped countries and their starving peoples. We must make sure that such aid gets to the people who really need it and is not deflected by corrupt officials into the black markets that are bound to flourish in some countries.

In this connection, Canadians should make it clear at the United Nations and elsewhere that we are fully aware of the stupendous problems confronting the Third World and of the hopes and aspirations of the peoples of the underdeveloped countries. We should support proposals for the development of "buffer stocks" in commodities and initiatives for raising living standards in such countries.

It is important to remember that large numbers of Canadians have their roots in Italy, in Germany, in Russia, in Poland, in Hungary and the other countries of Western and Eastern Europe. We should continue the initiatives taken by Prime Minister Trudeau to keep open the lines of communication with these and other countries. We must also work for trade arrangements with the European Economic Community, as well as with the Soviet Union and its satellites and with other countries. We should make a special effort to develop trading relationships with the countries of the Middle East.

But always we should keep in mind that over two-thirds of our trade, exports and imports, is with the United States. That is where our basic interests lie. That is where the basic aims of our foreign policy must be directed.

Chapter 10.

Summing Up

The world is facing dangerous and unhappy times that may include mass starvation and pestilence in some areas and possibly rebellions, increased terrorist activities, and even wars. The industrialized countries, including the United States, will be confronted with difficult social changes. These will occur as a result of shortages of oil and gas and other industrial raw materials that eventually will mean the end of long years of exponential rates of growth. However, insofar as the United States is concerned, this will probably not mean a reduction from a reasonably satisfactory level of economic activity for a long time to come. These adjustments, including the gradual acceptance of a different set of social and moral values, will mean changes in political attitudes and practices. Altogether, to use an expression of the airways, we face a long period of turbulence.

Canada will not escape these difficulties and changes. But, relatively speaking, we are in a fortunate position. We should not have to contend with either a population or a food problem. We have most of the industrial raw materials we need. In the next few years we may be short of oil and gas, but in the longer term we should be able to develop sufficient quantities of these and other energy sources.

If we wish to take full advantage of our relatively very favourable circumstances, we shall have to exercise greater wisdom than we have done in the past – or perhaps than it has been necessary for us to do in the past. For one thing, we may have to accept a slower rate of economic growth. If other industrialized countries have little growth they may reduce their requirements for some of the commodities we customarily export. To that extent, our imports may have to be reduced as well. Inevitably, this would reduce the steady growth rate of our GNP, to which we have become accustomed. But unless there is a world collapse, unless the system of international payments breaks down completely, I see no reason why Canada should not continue to prosper and to grow at a moderate rate. In doing so, I hope we shall give a high priority to the continued reduction of poverty in our own country while doing as much as we reasonably can to help the undeveloped nations whose plight may be truly desperate.

It would be the height of folly for Canada to adopt isolationist or protectionist policies. On the contrary, we should do everything possible, through our own initiatives or in supporting those of others, to re-establish international trading, payments, and other agreements that have broken down as well as the establishment of new ones. At the same time, we should not overlook the importance of thinking in terms of Canada for Canadians. By this, I mean we should stop the exploitation of Canadian resources, of all kinds, by and for the benefit of foreigners.

Some fifteen years ago, in speaking to the National Federation of Canadian University Students in Vancouver, I said:

... I am still optimistic about what Canada can accomplish over the long term if we manage our affairs intelligently. What we need, I think, is to agree upon the objectives that Canadians should aim for, and then to develop the policies that we should follow in an effort to achieve them. In thinking about a consistent set of policies, there are of course many different tests or yardsticks against which proposals can be measured.

For example:

1. Will they result in more jobs and less unemployment?
2. Will they cause inflation?
3. Will they make a real and substantial contribution to the defence of the Free World or of North America?
4. Will they result in a further loss of Canadian independence, or the reverse?
5. Will they benefit the people of Canada as a whole, or just particular groups or classes or sections of the country?
6. How will they affect personal incomes and the cost of living?
7. Will they tend to create difficulties for us at some future time?
8. Will they benefit people in depressed sections of Canada, or people in other countries who are less well off than we are?

After pointing out that all these tests are not mutually exclusive, I said:

But in deciding upon the best course for Canada to follow in the years immediately ahead, it seems to me there are two factors above all others that will be of paramount importance. In the first place, the threat of serious and possibly chronic unemployment is beginning to frighten or to haunt us . . . in the second place, as I have suggested, if we really do wish Canada to retain her separate identity as an independent nation, we will have to re-examine our present defence and foreign policies and do something about stopping and then reversing the trend under which such a staggering number of our most dynamic industries have fallen into foreign hands.

It follows from what I have been saying that, in considering the pros and cons of any policy proposals, there are two tests above all others that should be kept very much in mind. Will the proposed policy result in more jobs and less unemployment and will the proposed policy result in a further loss of Canadian independence, or the reverse?

I still believe just as firmly that our domestic policies should be subjected to these tests. Under present and foreseeable conditions there is another test that should be added. Will the proposed policy result in more or less inflation?

The proposals put forward in the preceding pages do meet these tests and, if implemented, should result in our economic affairs being managed in the best interests of Canadians. Let me summarize my principal proposals:

1. **To regain control of the economy**

A free vote should be taken in the House of Commons on a Resolution expressing the firm view that the ownership of all foreign-controlled companies over a certain size (there are only 32 of them according to my proposal) should be transferred to Canadians in stages over a period of ten years.

The advantages of this proposal would be:

(a) No legislation would be required and there would be no need for sanctions.
(b) Only 32 companies would be affected.
(c) The companies would not be nationalized.
(d) It would be left to the foreign owners to decide how the shares of their subsidiaries should be sold to Canadians.
(e) They would have plenty of time to work things out.

(f) The cost – to the Canadians who bought the shares of these 32 companies, not the government – would be about $15 billion over a period of ten years. This sum is quite within our financial capabilities.

(g) For all practical purposes, the transfer of ownership of these 32 large companies would resolve the foreign control issue.

2. The oil and gas industry

Control of all the larger foreign-controlled oil companies should be transferred to Canadians according to the formula referred to under Point 1 above. Failing that, all foreign-controlled oil companies – or at least Imperial Oil, the largest of them – should be taken over by the federal government and operated by a Crown Corporation on its behalf. No action should be taken respecting Canadian-controlled oil companies.

3. Balance of payments

It is imperative for us to reduce the Current Account deficits in our balance of payments, which in 1974 amounted to approximately $1.8 billion and which in 1975 may amount to between $4 and $5 billion. The following proposals are presented:

(a) Nothing should be done to slow the reduction in the value of the Canadian dollar in terms of the U.S. dollar. In this connection and for other reasons, interest rates in Canada should be reduced.

(b) Foreign-controlled companies in Canada, including those in the automotive industry, should be requested to develop domestic sources for parts and components now being imported – Ford of Canada should be requested to re-establish a fully functioning purchasing department in Canada. The Department of National Revenue should impose strict limits on the amount of management and service charges, etc., payable to foreign corporations that will be allowed as deductions for income tax purposes in Canada.

(c) The government should establish a national trading corporation to act on behalf of Canadian manufacturers and producers in dealing with countries, including the Arab countries, that would prefer to do business through such channels.

4. Monopolies and oligopolies

A permanent public body or commission should be established to review in advance proposed price increases in all industries that are structured along monopolistic or oligopolistic lines.

5. When the times call for stimulating the economy – the following policies are recommended:

(a) A reduction of taxes with emphasis on regressive taxes.

(b) Substantial subsidies for housing; for example, greatly reduced rates of interest on mortgages to first buyers of new dwelling units. (Quite apart from economic reasons, it is important to bring the price of housing within the reach of young households.)

(c) A relatively easy and steady monetary policy should be followed as a general rule.

(d) Interest rates should be reduced both to stimulate the economy and to restrain inflation.

(e) The value of the Canadian dollar should be reduced.

6. When the times call for restraining inflation—

Inflation of the severity we have been suffering from in the last two years or so must be taken with the utmost seriousness. The policies for combating inflation listed below are intended for periods when the rate of inflation is rising and has reached levels of about five per cent.

(a) The permanent price control machinery recommended in the case of monopolies and oligopolies should be extended temporarily to other key commodities and services.

(b) Under similar circumstances, the Food Prices Review Board should be empowered to supervise the prices of basic foodstuffs.

(c) There should be controls on rents.

(d) Depending on the state of the economy, the chartered banks should be restrained from making certain types of loans. For example, there should be some restrictions on consumer credit made either directly or indirectly.

(e) Interest rates should be reduced.

(f) Wage controls might not be acceptable or enforceable under present conditions even if price controls of the kind contemplated were introduced, but some government authority should indicate periodically the kind of wage increases that would be appropriate in various industries.

7. Banking

(a) From the time of Confederation until the last revision of the Bank Act in 1967, limits were placed on the rate of interest the chartered banks were permitted to charge their customers. These limits were removed in 1967. Some restriction should be re-imposed but on a somewhat more flexible basis than in the past. One suggestion would be to tie the permissible "prime rate" chargeable by the chartered banks from time to time to some percentage of the "Bank Rate" imposed by the Bank of Canada.

(b) In recent months, some 170 foreign banks have come

to Canada through the back door by incorporating Canadian subsidiaries under provincial legislation, often with little or no capital. All these operations should be brought under federal supervision and become subject to federal regulations.

8. Monetary Policy

A restrictive monetary policy should be avoided and the facilities of the Business Development Bank should be used to advantage.

9. Labour

If the public continues to be seriously inconvenienced, especially at a time of recession and much too high levels of unemployment, Parliament and the Provincial Legislatures should legislate against further strikes in the public services – especially fire and police protection, hospitals, transportation, postal and other essential services. In doing so, it would be important to take a sympathetic and understanding view of labour's legitimate interests – as well as those of the general public – and to provide procedures for arbitration that will make this clear.

10. Power and influence of the federal government

In the thirty years since the end of the war, the power of the federal government has been steadily eroded in favour of the provinces. It is time the pendulum began to swing the other way. To achieve this, the federal government should assert itself by taking the kind of initiatives in the economic field that are outlined in this book.

11. Responsibility for social security programs

At the same time, the federal government should stress its willingness to transfer to the provinces full responsibility both for the administration and the financing of all shared cost programs in the social security field with the exception of unemployment insurance and the Canada Pensions Plan.

12. Foreign Policy

Our foreign policy should be in phase with our economic policies. This means the main preoccupation should be with our many and varied relationships with the United States.

Taken together, these various proposals call for some major changes in our economic policies. How likely is this to happen? I do not know the answer to this question. But we do know the world is faced with new conditions which inevitably will mean important changes in the policies of other countries; some of these changes have already taken place. Canadians can wait like the ostrich with their heads in the sand until they are confronted with more of these disrupting changes and then attempt to react to them in an *ad hoc* manner. In that event, I believe there is a good chance that George Ball's prophecies will be borne out; that Canada, during some period of crisis, will be absorbed by the United States, perhaps without most Canadians fully realizing what was happening.

The alternative is for Canadians to recognize both the incipient threats and dangers of the world in which we live and also the opportunities that can be ours if we have the gumption – the courage and the will – to do the things necessary to ensure our independence. We shall also need the gumption – and the sense – to do the things that will be necessary if we are to manage our affairs in better fashion than we have done in the past.

I believe the time is ripe for the federal government to give the positive leadership that is needed. The Prime Minister has been doing this in our foreign relationships with considerable success. The time has come for similar initiatives in our domestic economic policies, especially those designed to recapture a greater degree of economic independence.